A NAZI
IN THE
FAMILY

A NAZI
IN THE
FAMILY

DEREK NIEMANN

First published in 2015 by Short Books
Unit 316, Screenworks
22 Highbury Grove
London N5 2ER

10 9 8 7 6 5 4 3 2 1

A CIP catalogue record for this book is available from the British Library.

ISBN 978-1-78072-222-1

Printed and bound in Great Britain by CPI Group (UK) Ltd,
Croydon, CR0 4YY

All images in this book © copyright the Niemann family, with the
exception of the photograph on page 288 © copyright Sarah Niemann.

The historic images have been scanned and digitally restored. Further
information about this process is given on page 262.

Introduction

"I was at Dachau. No, not as an inmate – I was one of the bad Germans. I used to tell people I was in Munich, but no, I was at Dachau." – Rudolf Adolf August Martin Wilhelm Niemann (my dad)

For most of his life, my father kept the story of his early childhood hidden away from the world, his children, even perhaps, from himself. Both he and his sister had left Germany for Scotland as young adults and it seemed they had closed a chapter of their lives, demonstrated most powerfully by the fact that they never spoke to each other in their native tongue. Though they had lived through the war in Nazi Germany, they never, ever, discussed it in front of us.

Very occasionally, I would hear my father and his sister talk of the parents they called *Vati* and *Mutti* (dad and mum). They spoke in tones of great warmth and affection that are typical of children for whom the death of a loved parent means endless bereavement.

I was 50 years old when, one April evening, the German grandfather who had died the year before I was born came unbidden into my house under a different guise. A casual search on the computer for something else brought the following words up on the screen:

SS-Hauptsturmführer Karl Niemann... crimes against humanity... use of slave labour.

My dad had told me that he thought his father was only a pen-pusher. And that was true. It was just that for seven years his pen pushed tens of thousands of half-starved concentration camp inmates from Auschwitz, Sachsenhausen, Buchenwald, Dachau and other places of shocking notoriety into work.

Eleven million people perished in the Holocaust. Most of them slept (and many died) in the bunk beds that my grandfather had responsibility for manufacturing. He regularly visited concentration camps as part of his work. He saw the skeletal figures and must surely have witnessed torture and brutality. Yet for ten years he carried on working for the SS regardless, taking home his wages, tending his garden, reinventing himself in the evenings as a family man.

A Berlin exhibition in 2013 named Karl Niemann as a *Schreibtischtäter*, a "desk-bound criminal". I came to discover that he was anything but desk-bound. And while the nature of his work was unquestionably criminal, my research led to a man whose actions and motivations were far more complex and even contradictory than I could ever have expected.

This book tries to follow and explain the life of my SS grandfather. But much more than that, it tells, through the voices of children of that time, an astonishing story of a family living through some of the most cataclysmic events of the twentieth century.

My father and his surviving brother broke their long silence for me, to give eyewitness testimonies. They had been mischief-making innocents who saw plenty and understood little. Whatever the sins of their father, I would not wish their experiences on anyone.

NIEMANN

FRIEDRICH ———————— **WILHELMINE**

WILHELM
GUSTAV
MINNA
JETTE
FRIEDRICH
AUGUST

KARL 1893–1960

'ANNE' ANNA–LUISE
1923–2010

'DIETER' ERNST-DIETRICH
1926–1945

ISABELLE

SCHWENKER

HEINRICH ———————————— **LINA**

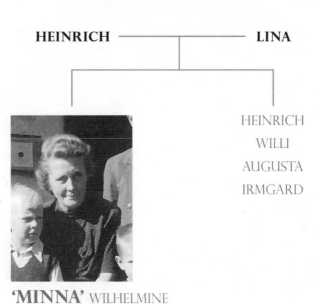

HEINRICH
WILLI
AUGUSTA
IRMGARD

'MINNA' WILHELMINE
1895–1960

'RUDI' RUDOLF
b1934

'EKI' EKART
b1938

MARTIN   DEREK   MICHAEL   KAI

Inklings

1

I was born into a land without mangoes. No pomegranates, paw-paws, kiwi fruits or clementines. No Lindt, Ferrero-Roché, or panettone. Scotland is a country whose umbilical cord is attached to a bag of sugar. Back in the 1960s, the choice of exotic delights from abroad was far more limited than it is today. But our family had its own private route to sweet ecstasy.

Every December, a taste of Germany arrived in a big cardboard box stamped with unpronounceable words of improbable length. The great opening drew out gingerbread biscuits dipped in thick white and dark chocolate. There was still more chocolate – little latticed affairs coated in crunchy multi-coloured beads. Best of all was the chocolate-covered marzipan, wrapped in red tin foil, and then wrapped again in cellophane, as if to protect its special qualities. "From Lübeck," said my dad, pronouncing the first syllable "eeooo" as if it was shooting off a ski slope. "The finest marzipan in the world." And it was too – the first bite releasing a delicate flavour of almonds. Then there was what my dad called "sshhtollen", an icing-dusted cake with a generous layer of marzipan and a fruity thick dough that you could squeeze with your tongue against the roof of your mouth. Hark the German angels sing.

Some of my earliest experiences introduced me to sounds from my father's homeland. He entered into the Christmas spirit, uttering four words that I came to know if not quite understand. He rolled his eyes, began conducting an invisible choir with both index fingers and half spoke, half incanted the words "*Stille Nacht, heilige Nacht*", his face a picture of reverential bliss.

My happiest moments as a small child came when he would once in a while prop me up on his knees facing him, holding me by the armpits. He began to sing a German nursery rhyme that appeared to have a plot like that of Humpty Dumpty, but with the bonus of a spine-tingling ending. "*Hoppe, hoppe Reiter, wenn er fällt dann schreit er*" (Bumpety, bump, rider, when he falls, he cries). It was a jiggling journey full of mounting suspense, for the hapless horseman does not fall off his horse and into a ditch until the very end. My dad would bounce me on his knee, his rhythmic chanting in that strange tongue, foreign and familiar, quickening until the moment when he shouted "*Plumpfs!*" and "dropped" me between his knees so that my bottom kissed the ground. Then he would always lift me up laughing. "Do it again, Daddy. Again." But he never would. I saw his broad smile fade, the enchantment vanish.

For the most part, Germany to us children meant the side that had lost the war. Action films played out on our black and white television every Saturday night. *The Battle of Britain*, *The Great Escape*, *Where Eagles Dare*, *The Dam Busters*... My dad seemed to watch willingly enough, eyes fixed to the screen, hand reaching into a bowl of peanuts. He dipped again, and again, and again. At the end of every film he would give the same pronouncement. If it was a British-made film, he would say: "Those bad Germans again." If it was American, he would lean back into the settee and declare: "Vot a load of utter rubbish."

If a programme about the First World War came on, my dad

would often be prompted to remark: "Vati got the Iron Cross." The corners of his by now tight-lipped mouth would curl downwards and he would pull out his left breast pocket between his thumb and forefinger, looking down as if he half expected to see the metal badge on his chest. "What did he get it for?" I asked hopefully. He shrugged. "I don't know. He didn't talk about it."

A war-obsessed boy, I was disappointed with my parents, who had lived through the Second World War, without it apparently leaving much trace on them. My mum had clearly had a dull, dull war, a small child crouching in the stairwell of her Glasgow tenement every night, waiting for the bombs to come, though she had been too young to remember when they did. Her father was Wee Willie Coulter, just 5 feet 3 inches tall, wearing a pork-pie hat and a long coat that came down to his shins and made him look like a KGB agent. Our Scottish grandfather hadn't even fought, but had been in a reserved occupation, keeping the Glasgow buses going with his spanner. My mum seemed to think he had been in the Home Guard… but she couldn't be sure what he'd done to defend his country.

Three years older than my mother, my dad would divulge only one brief memory of his life in Berlin, and would do so with such Pavlovian predictability that I was sure it was the only memory he possessed; the single recollection of a very small boy. He spoke of watching pieces of tin foil raining down on the city – a ruse by the Allied planes overhead to disrupt German radar, he said. He also told me that his family had escaped to the Alps. His father had been a banker… he had taught his sons to light the tips of fresh pine needles to fill the house with a sweet aroma.

Out of these fragments I pieced together a truly unremarkable wartime life – the family evacuated to sit out a rustic existence in a little Bavarian town, father keeping the books in the local bank, a cuckoo clock on the wall, a log fire in the grate, the whole drama passing the family by.

Not quite. He did tell us his older brother Dieter had fought and died in the war: "In the Panzers, the tanks, you know. They were all killed, all but one. He was just a boy." "How old was he – fifteen, sixteen, seventeen?" "I don't know."

Long after the war, my dad had followed his big sister to the promised land that was the mining belt of Lanarkshire, south of Glasgow. Her name was written Anne, though it was said as "Ann-uh". That wasn't even her real name – on the day of her funeral I learned from the priest's sermon that my aunt had been born Anna-Luise. My dad used neither of these names, but always called his sister "Nuschen". "Did the name mean anything?" "No."

Ja, my father a strange and particularly German way of constructing sentences had, but Aunt Anne's accent was something else, a glorious fusion of German and broad Lanarkshire. "Ve vull no be doin' vat," she would say, stooping a little and shaking her tight, permed mass of blonde curls for emphasis.

At Aunt Anne's, everything German was best – she cooked us heavy (and delicious) German meals and we sat at the end of the room around a table made of heavy German oak. We were ushered into ornately carved German chairs that were so heavy we had to dive under the table and slide up into them, or climb over the arms and parachute down into the seats, rather than attempt to move them. The grown-ups drank German wine: Anne said Riesling was the finest, though I think they only ever poured out bottles of cut-price Liebfraumilch from cut glasses (German, of course). Beethoven (or was it Wagner?) was better than the Beatles.

Even the dog was Teutonic, a fierce-looking German shepherd with a roar for a bark. "Major" belonged to Uncle George, a Scottish coalman with a mass of coal-black hair and a staccato machine-gun-fire way of speaking, who had married Aunt Anne after the war and brought her back to his home town of Larkhall.

The third of the German-born siblings lived on our wall, in a chest of drawers, and in a cage. Uncle Ekart was an intriguing mixture – a bohemian artist, a window dresser and a sign writer, and all the more interesting for being absent, since he had stayed behind in Germany while his brother and sister left for Scotland. We had somehow acquired one of his paintings – a Picassoesque picture of what looked like a deer licking its own genitals. It hung on the dining-room wall until, by a process of embarrassment and relegation over the years, it was last remembered under a pile of football programmes in my brother's wardrobe.

Photographs provided evidence that Ekart had been to visit us in the mid-60s and had dressed us little children in flamboyant native American costumes that he had made especially for us. In one black and white print, my little self appears squinting under a headdress of goose feathers. Uncle Eki brought us presents of lederhosen too. We ran round the garden in our thick leather shorts, but – though I did not know it at the time – my mum would never let us wear them beyond the front gate for fear of what people might say… what they might find out about us.

In a corner of our living room was a bird cage, where a mute budgerigar called Eki perched. The bird had none of the glamour of its namesake, for the rare photographs we had showed a man with the looks of film star Yves Montand. His wife Ulla was every bit as beautiful, a dead ringer for the vivacious Princess Margaret in her youth. They were young, they were tanned, they were glamorous. They were not of us, with our sugar-rotted teeth, black fillings, peelie-wally white skin and ill-matched clothes.

The fourth sibling was propped up on Aunt Anne's sideboard. It was the only photograph in her house, as I remember – a side view of a blonde teenage boy wearing what looked like some kind of Boys' Brigade uniform. Since it had always been there, and was therefore never subjected to a child's scrutiny and inquisition of the new, I never paid it much notice. Out of sight of Anne, my parents told me this was her brother – and also my father's brother. His name was Dieter. "Oh, the Dieter who…?" "Yes, he died in the war. No, I don't know how old…"

And what of my German grandparents? As a young bride, my mother had stayed in Hameln* with her in-laws. She provided cameo one-liners to me about her time there that were enough to satisfy my tepid curiosity. Though my mum spoke no German, she had picked up enough to remember the one question that her elderly, absent-minded mother-in-law would ask repeatedly: "*Wo ist meine Brille?*" (Where are my glasses?). She recalled that her father-in-law did not even have a speaking part. "He just sat in the corner in his chair." I thought of the one memory I had of my Scottish great-grandfather in East Kilbride, propped up in his seat with a blanket round his legs. Old people were just that. Old. They didn't do much.

In the 1970s, all three siblings suffered life-changing blows. It was the decade when my dad sank into some of his deepest struggles against depression. We had moved to Hatfield, just north of London. Though he had been a skilled toolmaker, and was still always making things with his hands, his job had gone with the virtual collapse of British engineering and he was now reduced to the deeply unsatisfying role of a lowly office clerk.

Though his hair would stay sandy-coloured until well into his sixties, his mind had sunk into an unfulfilled middle age. I watched my father give broad chimpanzee grins, and see behind them

---

* The north German town is often spelt Hamelin in English.

desperation in his eyes, conflict in his face. We did not understand what it meant and in those days, nobody spoke about mental illness. For him there were long silent evenings in front of the television, and too many days spent alone in his garage. He was prone to throwing out one-liners that didn't make sense and then retreating back into muteness. "Anne's furniture came from a concentration camp," he offered once. In the context of nothing, it was too outlandish, too absurd to be taken seriously.

One night, when I was thirteen years old, my dad did not come back from work. The police found him in his crashed car a hundred miles north and told my mother he had mumbled to them that he was on his way back to Scotland. But where was he really going? I remember sitting in a stately home tearoom with him a little while after he had had a spell in a hospital psychiatric unit. Someone irked him somehow – maybe they banged against his chair. He gave the man a torrent of abuse – all in German. That incident seemed to encapsulate a problem. It wasn't just that my dad didn't seem to be in the same room as his family – in his head, he wasn't even in the same country.

An attempt was made in our early teenage years to bring my father closer to his two sons and his heritage. We were each given a lined notebook and he began to teach us German. *Das Messer* – the knife. *Die Gabel* – the fork. *Der Löffel* – the spoon. Gabel, liffle, piffle. Our dad was no teacher and we were reluctant pupils, uninspired by learning by rote and lured elsewhere by our school work, pop music, TV and football. The initiative died on the second page of our new vocabulary book.

We visited our Onkel Ekart just once as a family, in the summer before my thirteenth birthday. It was a blazing hot Hameln on the river Weser, the Pied Piper town. While Eki's house was amazing, with split levels and a sun terrace, it was distinctly chilly in spirit. My uncle's marriage was in difficulties, my two cousins badly behaved, my own parents mired in their own troubles. I had no real sense of my uncle's character – his English was limited, his wife scarcely bothered to try. My dad was the lone interpreter. And he was deaf in one ear.

In the years that followed, estrangement between the already distant families deepened: even the exchange of cards and presents at Christmas stopped. Then, in quick succession, my uncle lost his job, his wife through divorce, and, after a terrible accident in which his car rolled and rolled, his right eye.

In 1974, Anne gained a grandchild, but lost her husband in a freak accident only a few weeks later. Every summer after that, she would come down to stay with us for a few weeks, and as I left the self-absorbed teenage years and entered early adulthood, I began to notice strange character traits in her. Though my widowed aunt was kind and patient, she never laughed once, or even smiled. The world of the perpetually disappointed seems to narrow and narrow. Aunt Anne talked incessantly about the minutiae of her daughter's life and, in time, the lives of her granddaughters too. But she had nothing of substance to say about her own existence. It was as if she had no life. And she moaned about petty injustices – the woman next door who got a benefit that she didn't, the council's slowness in coming to decorate her house, the buses that were always late.

Strangest of all to me, everything that she was given she accepted without showing any semblance of gratitude. We once took her down to London to a Proms concert, and sat beside the double basses as they beat the pulse of Stravinsky's *Rite of Spring*. It was one of the most exhilarating nights of my life. Anne left the Albert Hall as if she had just gone to the supermarket and found it had run out of milk. No matter what she was given, she received it with the same doleful, silent acceptance.

I suppose it must have been in the late 70s or early 80s that the media focus on Germany switched. Britain seemed to tire of reliving battle victories in films to make it feel better about itself and turned to Germany's role in a word that we heard for the first time then – the Holocaust. During my first summer vacation from Manchester University, I had gone to work as a waiter in the Swiss Alps and periodically rang my parents from a public call box beside a mountain stream. I spoke to my dad on a June day when snow fell:

"I'm going to your country for a couple of days tomorrow. I thought I'd head to Munich and pay a visit to Dachau to see what your lot got up to."

"I was at Dachau."

"You were at Dachau? The concentration camp?"

"Yes but no, not as an inmate – I was one of the bad Germans. I used to tell people I was in Munich, but no, I was at Dachau. My father was working there... just a pen-pusher." He closed up. There was nothing more he had to say on the subject.

Two days later, I followed the mundane routine of catching a bus from Dachau railway station to the concentration camp. A friend had visited Auschwitz and she said that no birds sang there. But there were plenty in good voice behind the barbed wire at this camp on that late-spring day in Bavaria. There was a fake shower room too where prisoners would have been gassed, except that the signs said the chamber had not been used. There were broad strips of gravel where camp huts were said to have been situated. But where was my grandfather in all this? Where was the office desk he might have sat behind, absorbed in shifting pieces of paper about while unspeakable acts of brutality took place all around him?

The memories of that camp would fade and my father's outburst would seem to have been just that. He never mentioned Dachau again and I would sometimes wonder if he had been muddled or simply trying to provoke a reaction. But a pall of uncertainty hung around the doings of my ancestors. My dad's middle name was Adolf and he had been born in 1934, the year after Hitler came to power. From time to time, he would say: "My father was a true Nazi. He believed in Hitler until he found out all the bad things. He was a disappointed man." How could a Nazi be anything but evil? I wanted to know more, but I didn't want to hear it. Though I had nominally reached the age of adulthood and university, I was still a self-indulgent teenager with teenage anxieties. I thought I was swimming in guilt over possible family connections with the most hideous of crimes. More likely, I was just guilty about my own inadequacies.

An example of that muddled guilt revealed itself shortly after I returned to university for my second year. I was invited to an odd thing – a Sunday afternoon party. Even more strange was the fact that I wasn't quite sure who had sent the invitation. I turned up at a spacious Edwardian student house, and only twigged that something was horribly wrong when, standing self-consciously within a circle of young men seeking common ground, I found the conversation turning to sharing stories of Bar Mitzvahs. One by one, the laughing boys told their tales and I felt a rising sense of shame and an invisible pointer swinging my way. I made my toilet excuses and left the room, fled the house, my jackboot trainers pounding all the way down the garden path. I never knew why I was invited to that party – on reflection I concluded someone had seen the name ending in –mann and wanted to invite a fellow Jew to the party.

One winter, at about the same time, my brother Martin and I went to stay with Aunt Anne for a long weekend and shared a bed on a mattress so soft that we woke up in the middle of the night having rolled in together. I had arrived the day before my brother and found myself alone with my aunt for the first and only time in my life. We sat in front of a blazing gas fire, the coiled elements glowing red, fake flames flickering, while in a painting above the mantelpiece, great waves waited to crash on the shore, as they had done in that picture for as long as I could remember, though the sea and sky had darkened, stained by decades of nicotine. To the side of the fireplace was a brass ornament, a pair of gold hands clasped in prayer.

I broached the subject of the war and, to my surprise, Anne began to open up and talk about her life in Berlin. My mother once said that Anne "only spoke about happy things", and it was true. For a while, she chattered about queuing for food and visits to the cinema and the theatre with her brother Dieter. Without a thought, I asked: "What happened to Dieter?" Anne paused, lowered her head slightly and looked up at me with sad, wary eyes: "He vos on the big guns, the ack-ack. One night there vos an explosion and Dieter, he turned to his best friend and found him on the ground… no head. After that, he had enough. He vent to join the Panzers and then – it vos just before the end of the var – he vos killed. Vee found out… there vos only vun survivor of his unit." We both stared into the fire for a minute or two in sombre reflection. "What was Dieter like?" I asked. She looked at me and lifted her eyebrows. "Vot voz he like? He vos like you, Dairrik. Aye, Dieter. He voz like you."

A little later the same evening, she was emboldened to remark that Derek was the Scottish equivalent of Dieter. Had I been named for him? I wondered. I quizzed my parents: they thought it was just a coincidence and said the name was a random choice. However, never again could I look at Anne without thinking she was staring back at a reincarnation of her dead brother. And I began to construct a fantasy character of my uncle, my doppelgänger – the heroic anti-

Nazi, the reluctant soldier, a figure to both look up to and pity for a life cut short.

During the period when I got married and raised a son, my dad's mental health recovered and my own concerns about our family background receded as they became less tangible. We even made light of them. My wife Sarah joked that my pedigree was "half Gorbals, half Goebbels", and teased her father-in-law about the shape of German army helmets, suggesting that they looked like turtles. Sometimes she made inadvertently funny comments: "Rudi's new shed is much better than I thought it would be. It's not jerry-built."

Back in Scotland, Anne's lifelong smoking habit continued in secret against doctor's orders. The tough old lady, a secret tippler too, died in 2010, at the age of 86. Shortly after her death, I began reading a newly published book called *Berlin at War*. Author Roger Moorhouse told a riveting story anchored in the recollections of ordinary people living in the city through those extraordinary times. I rang my father to tell him some of the eyewitness stories about the bombing raids on the city, expecting him to reel off the old chestnut about showers of tin foil falling from the skies. But he launched off on a wholly unexpected tack:

"*Ja*, I remember standing outside and seeing them up there. Huge great things, Flying Fortresses. I was watching one of them and then it disappeared. Hit. Exploded. Gone. Just like that."

"You saw that happen? You saw the planes being shot out of the sky?"

"Yes. Of course."

"Then you remember things about the war, about what happened in Berlin?"

"I remember many things. Some day I will tell you about them," came the enigmatic, irresistible answer.

It seemed that his sister's death had unlocked something in my father. It was as if he now had permission to speak. And before long, as we sat in his bungalow overlooking the North Sea, and I listened to his stories, I marvelled that nearly 50 years of my own life had passed without me knowing anything of what he was telling me.

The account that my father gave me that day was compelling, but not just for the extraordinary tales he told. They were the recollections of a child, and I began to realise that they had remained so. Perhaps the memories had been repressed too long, and perhaps he had left Germany too young for them to be subjected to recalibration through the experiences and understanding of mature adulthood. Here was the naïve, unvarnished, and authentic voice of an eleven-year-old boy spoken by a man in his late seventies.

It would be another eighteen months before a much more sinister angle intruded on my father's story. My wife was due to attend a conference in Berlin and I decided to go along for the ride. "I'll look up your old house while I'm there," I told my dad. "Berlin-Zehlendorf, Dienstweg Neunzehn," he fired off in an instant. "That was our address. But it's not called that now. That was the old Nazi name for my street."

Just a few days before we left for Germany, I was still hunting for information. I typed "Berlin Zehlendorf Dienstweg" into the computer to see if by chance there was anything about the street where he had lived. The name "Karl Niemann" came up on the first screen. My grandfather's name. I clicked. And there was my grandfather listed in a position, a terrible position of authority and the words *crimes against humanity* and *use of slave labour* on the same page swimming before my eyes. I found him in online papers relating to the Nuremberg trials. In Berlin itself, I went to the Topography of Terror Museum on the site of the Gestapo headquarters and found his name in archives and state documents. He appeared in books about slave labour and genocide. He was little more than a footnote in history, but what a footnote.

I did go to my father's old house, at the very end of the *U-Bahn* line. I had not expected beauty, serenity and nestboxes. Woodpeckers chipped from trees all around. A roadside stall was selling honey. The houses, wonderfully rustic, had been planted within a forest of pines. The house at Dienstweg 19 was dark inside and apparently empty. I photographed front and back. A man in the street looked suspiciously and asked if he could help me. He didn't mean what he was saying. But when I explained my story, he brightened. He said my German was very good. It wasn't.

I began writing a note for the absent occupants of the house, giving them the names of its first occupants. I was about to drop it through the letterbox, when a youngish, dark-haired woman came up – she lived in that very house. I reeled off my story once again. At first, she looked uncertain, but then she had an impulsive change of mind, rushed forward and let me inside, introducing me to her father. He showed me round, allowed me to take photographs of the living room, dining room, kitchen, hall, cellar and back garden. "There was a bomb shelter there... somewhere," I said doubtfully, inspecting a bush and a short, level lawn. We sat down and I told him what I knew of the family's life in his house. Eventually, I owned up: "I'm afraid my grandfather was in the SS." "Of course," he said. "You could not live on this estate unless you were in the SS."

In the space of just over a year, I was to visit Germany three times. The greatest help during that period came from Karl's youngest son, my uncle Ekart, who is the living antithesis of everything Hitler stood for. He votes for a party the Nazis banned and he and his wife Adelheid semi-adopted two Ukranian children, victims of the Chernobyl nuclear accident, children who would have been classified by the regime his father supported as *Untermenschen* (sub-human).

All through the process of researching and writing this book, I learned to trust no one, not even myself. Besides the inevitable distortions, confusions and lapses of memory through the long passage of time, there were also other considerations – the natural biases that a family will put on the doings of its own. What follows is the truest account I can give, the story of my SS grandfather and his family.

The Pied Pipers

2

Legend has it that in the Middle Ages, the town of Hameln was afflicted by a plague of rats. A stranger dressed in multi-coloured clothes appeared and offered to rid the town of its burden. The so-called pied piper played his magic flute and drew the rats out of the houses and down to the river Weser, where they all drowned. But when the people reneged on their agreement to pay the piper for his services, he exacted a terrible revenge, enticing the children of the town away, never to be seen again.

In the first week of August 1914, a different piper played a different tune, although the result was much the same. He lured the young men of Hameln and the surrounding villages out of their houses and down to the railway station. They climbed into carriages and were taken away. More than 3,000 of them were never to be seen again.

One of the eager young recruits who went to war that summer was a sandy-haired man of average height and average build, sporting the regulation Charlie Chaplin moustache. Twenty-one-year-old Karl Niemann signed up as an officer cadet with the 4th Hannoverian Infantry Regiment in the week war was declared. Like millions of other instant soldiers throughout Europe, he was expecting a quick result. Men of his grandfather's generation had fought short and victorious land-grabbing campaigns for Prussia against Denmark, Austria and France. Now his regiment was going to fight for a unified Germany, and surely the result would be the same? Paris by Christmas, they said. The other side said Berlin by Christmas. How many of the young men of Hameln looked at the memorial in the town cemetery and pondered over the long list of the dead from the short Franco-Prussian war of only a few decades before?

The day after Karl became a soldier, he was in a train passing through Hannover, Bremen, Cologne and Aachen, picking up more volunteers in new uniforms at each city. A little way out of Aachen, the train halted at a stop in wooded country on the border. The disgorged soldiers were about to defend their country by invading neutral Belgium. They marched for 185 miles in scorching heat until, just two weeks and a day after he had signed up, Karl was fighting his first battle.

Karl Friedrich Wilhelm Niemann began his life in rather unpromising circumstances on 30th April 1893, in the hamlet of Hemeringen, a few miles of rolling country outside Hameln. His father, Friedrich, was a miller; Karl was the seventh and youngest child. His eldest brother Wilhelm would follow his father's career in the mill, another brother was "Baker Fritz", and another ended up running a hotel.

At the bottom of the heap, Karl had an additional disadvantage that neither of his surviving sons would know the truth about until late in life. They had thought, or had been led to believe, that Karl's left hand had been maimed during the First World War. "It was always bent, it was hit somehow. You wouldn't look at it, you know," recalled his son, Rudi. But there is no mistaking that in the portrait photograph taken in the week Karl joined the army, the left hand grasping hold of his gloves in a standard military pose has significantly shorter fourth and fifth fingers. The origin of this congenital deformity was kept hidden from his children, though the defect was there for all to see.

A good student, adept with figures, Karl was sent after his schooling to work in town, apprenticed to the Hannoversche Bank, a Hameln sub-branch of the Deutsche Bank. Though he spent the rest of his life living in towns and cities, he would always keep his country ways, drawing the sap from silver birch trees and using it to anoint his hair as a kind of sweet-smelling sticky lacquer, taking conifer branches indoors and lighting the tips as a rustic air freshener, weeing on plants in the garden to help them grow. He was a generally mild-mannered, obliging man, thrifty to the point of being frugal. But beneath the watermark of affability, he possessed a strong, unbending streak of stubbornness.

Hameln town was deemed too far for Karl to walk or ride from his birthplace on a daily commute, so he took lodgings with his sister Wilhelmine and her extrovert husband Friedrich Schmidt in a narrow medieval lane called Fischpfortenstrasse. The timber-framed house at number 11 was full to bursting – the Schmidts' fifth child was born in August 1912, the month Karl moved in – and they were always short of money. Friedrich "Pappen" Schmidt was a *Malermeister* (master painter) and his wife chided him to "paint walls, not people; they earn us more money."

A regular visitor to their house was seventeen-year-old Wilhelmine "Minna" Schwenker, an itinerant dressmaker from the other side of the Weser, who had built up a reputation as a thrifty seamstress: "Give her a handkerchief and she will make you a suit," it was said of her. Minna came to the house to mend clothes and make new ones for the growing family. Cunning Pappen Schmidt saw matchmaking opportunities for his young brother-in-law and would make a point of saying on evenings when she worked late in Fischpfortenstrasse: "Karl, would you please accompany Miss Schwenker home?"

Minna Schwenker was the daughter of a ship captain who held the eye-popping title of *Oberweserdampfschifffahrtsgesellschaftkapitän*. Heinrich Schwenker had plied his steamship between Hameln and Bremen. The ship captains of the Weser each earned enough from their trade to have a three-storey house built on a plot of land a short distance from the water's edge. The line of ship captains' houses was named Adolfstrasse. Having made his fortune, Heinrich raised a family: "I made my money and now my children spend it," he would boast. Poor Minna was the Cinderella of the family, the youngest child, whose mother would announce to guests: "These are my children – Heinrich, Wilhelm, Augusta… oh, and Minna."

What Minna did to deserve her mother's offhand cruelty was never explained, except that, like Karl, she was born with a slight deformity – a pronounced squint in her right eye. And she had a faulty heart valve that sometimes left her breathless and, throughout her life, short of energy. When Minna was fourteen, she gained a sister. It seems she developed a way of coping with feelings of rejection by lavishing affection on the child. It was a character trait that would last throughout her life. The woman with an overriding desire to protect those she loved walked home with the man who possessed a bedrock of obstinacy. They were ordinary characteristics in a perfectly normal couple. And under ordinary circumstances, these traits would probably have never amounted to anything much.

Perhaps the two young people who crossed the river together were bound by acceptance of each other's frailty; in any case, they fell in love very quickly. They took romantic walks along the Weser and canoodled on riverside benches, sometimes, as Karl recalled wryly, watched through field glasses by the town's peeping Tom.

The couple were already engaged when war broke out. And since Karl was still only an impecunious apprentice at the bank, it was not likely that they would be married very soon.

The German army – with Karl somewhere in the middle – advanced to within just 27 miles of Paris. A million of the city's inhabitants left the capital, including every member of the cabinet, showing solidarity with their fleeing *citoyens*. Meanwhile, the retreating French army retreated no more and dug in around the river Marne. Fortified trenches and coils of barbed wire along a largely static front were to be the nature of warfare for the next four years, bloody battles interspersed with long periods of tedious inaction.

Many years later, surrounded by his family, Karl would have rare expansive moods in which he would tell one and a half stories of his wartime exploits. The first story captured the absurdity of his situation. Ekart remembered him telling how the Germans and the French positioned themselves in protective trenches opposite each other for months at a time. They didn't go forwards and they didn't go back. Between the fronts flowed a stream. In this situation, the opponents reached a peaceable agreement. From 8am until midday, the Germans collected their drinking water from the stream. And from 1pm until 6pm, the French collected theirs. Presumably, for the rest of the time, they blasted away at each other.

Karl grew animated when telling his second story, acting out the part, holding a half-raised imaginary rifle in his hands: "It was a pitch-black night and we could hear the enemy coming, but we could not see him. And then, all of a sudden, the moon came out from behind the clouds and there he was. I lifted my rifle, pointed it at him, and –" "That'll do, Karl. The children don't want to hear any of this," interrupted Minna, in a voice that brooked no argument. "But we did!" exclaimed the white-bearded Eki, his eyes still gleaming with the memory of frustration at a gripping tale of his boyhood cut short. Karl often hummed the Radetzky March, "ta-ta, tum ti tum, ta-ta tum ti tum". "It was my father's regimental march," said Rudi.

The bare facts show that Karl experienced some of the worst of the fighting. He fought at Arras, Ypres, and, in just two days on the Somme, his regiment lost more than 1,100 men. Karl was awarded the Iron Cross Second Class, but so too were four and a half million others. The medal was supposed to be awarded for bravery – it was almost as if it was dished out to those who had made it through a battle alive. He received the Iron Cross First Class too, for being alive that bit longer. In 1916, he was made an officer and the newly entitled Leutnant Niemann jumped on a train to spend eight days' leave in Hameln, where his playful fiancée Minna dressed up in his military tunic and peaked officer's cap and posed for her picture.

Karl's luck ran out – or perhaps it began – on 31st July 1917, the first day of an offensive that came to be known variously as the Third Battle of Ypres, Passchendaele and – a name coined by British Prime Minister David Lloyd George – "the battle of the mud". A two-centimetre deluge of rain fell on that day and, after a dawn barrage of fire, the British and French armies advanced farther than they had in nearly three years, capturing 5,000 German soldiers in just three days. The artist Otto Dix portrayed the horror of that confrontation with an illustration of a wounded German soldier carried by his comrades on a makeshift stretcher, a blanket strung between two poles, rain teeming down around the bedraggled and dejected soldiers. Karl was one of those on a stretcher. He was wounded and then taken prisoner in a place called Houthoulsterwald.

Though the nature of Karl's injuries is not known, his next destination is recorded. He was taken far from the action to Châteauneuf-d'Ille-et-Vilaine, a prisoner-of-war camp deep in the heart of rural Brittany. He spoke a little to Rudi about his experiences there:

"My father said that this prisoner-of-war camp was run by the Catholic Church, and he got very good treatment because they always want to make you a Catholic, so they treat you nicely. But the women on the outside – they used to come up and show them what they thought of them by lifting their skirts up, pulling their knickers down and showing them the arse!"

Official records show that the German officers were cared for by nuns and taken out to work on local farms under light supervision. They received irregular mail from home too – Karl pinned up an oval studio photograph of Minna that he was sent for his birthday – but they were nevertheless still prisoners. Karl never learned his captors' language – he would always be limited to what he admitted to be "schoolboy French". The war ended with Germany's defeat in November 1918. Did they go home? No, they spent that Christmas in Brittany, and the Christmas after. They "celebrated" New Year's Day 1920 still in French captivity.

These men paid doubly for Germany's defeat. Under the terms of the Armistice, prisoners of war belonging to the Entente (Britain, France and their allies) were freed immediately hostilities ceased. But the Allies decreed that German prisoners would only be released after peace terms had been settled under the Treaty of Versailles. The Red Cross negotiated with the Allied Supreme Council right through 1919, asking repeatedly for the men to be repatriated. It was not until March 1920, fully sixteen months after the end of the war, that Karl was finally set free.

Nearly 27 years old, Karl returned to Hameln. Even then, a good while after the war was over, the town was still festering with resentment and it was largely directed at Hameln's small Jewish community. People had rounded on the Jews of the town during a nationwide financial crisis in 1873. Once more, blame was being heaped on the guiltless Jews – this time for Germany's capitulation in the war. The antagonism was such that it brought a reaction.

The Jewish community put up a bronze plaque in the synagogue "to the memory of our fallen sons". The preacher and teacher of the community, Salomon Bachrach, spoke proudly and angrily at the inauguration ceremony:

> *No one has the right to say the German Jew failed his duty in war. On our memorial plaque are six names. Every Jewish community in our country can put up such memorials, and on each are names of fallen Jews. We do not tolerate their memory being besmirched... we are in spirit before a single large grave. Those who slumber inside are Germany's sons. They died for us. We greet them at this hour, the brave, who are bound to us and our German fatherland with bonds of love and loyalty.*

It was a moving, eloquent rebuff. But who was listening outside the synagogue?

Karl, the returning son, was welcomed back to his job at the Hannoversche Bank, where he had been promoted to the giddy heights of clerk, and was embraced by his beloved and loyal Minna. They married in the town's Münsterkirche on 26th November 1921. Minna would often point out that their courtship had lasted nine full years. Eki called his parents' relationship "a great love". They had suffered the first of a number of long separations that would mark their lives together and apart.

One feature of Karl's character that survived the war was a strong, uncompromising nationalism. It surfaced from time to time, most notably when his brother-in-law Heinrich came up in conversation. Bremen barge captain Heinrich Schwenker had served in the navy and was one of the sailors who had quite deliberately sunk their own fleet at the Orkney harbour of Scapa Flow in 1919, to prevent the ships falling into British hands. Karl was unbending in his condemnation: "A good German would not have done that," he declared bluntly, and often.

If there is one remarkable feature of Karl's unremarkable life in the 1920s, it is – given his later career – an apparent complete absence of political engagement. Nearly all of those who rose within the SS during the 1930s to positions of power had a benchmark of commitment from the previous decade. Many joined one of the paramilitary groups that sprang up to back a range of right-wing parties. Half a million war veterans and those too young to fight were members of the Stahlhelm, Bund der Frontsoldaten (Steel Helmet, League of Frontline Soldiers), supporting the German National People's Party. Karl was not. By 1930, there were about 100,000 men belonging to the Sturmabteilung (SA), also known as the stormtroopers. Karl was not one of them. And nor was he a member of their parent political party, the Nationalsozialistische Deutsche Arbeiterpartei, the Nazi Party, which had been founded in the month after he returned from France. In fact, if the numerous official forms that he filled in before, during and after the war are to be believed, Karl belonged to nothing at all, though his son Eki had a feeling that he was an active member of a club for card players.

The uneventful life of a bank clerk was played out over the next two years, during which Minna became pregnant with their first child. Karl's boss would file the following report: "In January 1923, he was given full control over the bank because of his diligence and good character. He was loved and respected by his co-workers. Herr

Niemann left the Hannoversche Bank on 30th Sept 1923 in order to further his education."

What Karl's boss August Meier meant by "to further his education" ("um sich weiter fortzubilden") is not known. Both of his sons had the vague recollection that Karl left the bank to take up a better-paid post at a Jewish-owned bank. It was a time when everyone was better paid, their incomes doubling, trebling, quadrupling by the day, though their escalating wages bought them less and less. Germany was suffering from the worst hyperinflation of any economy in history.

Karl was bringing his pay home in a wheelbarrow. On the day Minna gave birth to Anna-Luise (Anne), a US dollar was worth 65 billion marks. A day later, it was worth 130 billion. Exactly a week after Anne's birth, Hitler attempted a coup in Munich (the infamous Beer Hall Putsch). One of his 2,000 armed supporters paid two billion marks of stolen money for their services, a future colleague of Karl's, was a seventeen-year-old called Karl Bestle.

Anne was born into a country on the verge of economic collapse. The Allies had imposed crippling post-war reparations on Germany, a nation already carrying the burden of war debts. Failure to meet its repayments caused France to send in troops to occupy the industrial region of the Ruhr at the beginning of the year. By November 1923, shops were hoarding food and in cities such as Dresden there were food riots. For Karl, a man whose whole professional life had been based on financial probity and who was now bringing a child into the world, the experience must have left a lasting impact.

The German economy recovered. The international community agreed a financial package called the Dawes Plan that staged reparations payments and, for the next few years, though ministers of the Weimar Republic came and went with startling regularity, Germany experienced a period of stability.

In Hameln, the Niemann family appeared to be going through their own period of stability too. Numerous photographs from that time show a pretty blonde girl with big bows in her hair, later pictured beside an even blonder baby brother. Ernst-Dietrich, ever after known as Dieter, was born on 23rd January 1926. The children are always smiling at the photographer, their father, sometimes playing together in the garden, sometimes posing with their mother. The family often took trips out to see their aunts and uncles in the countryside, Anne and Dieter mounted on huge horses, riding in great haycarts, or draping their arms around various and sundry cousins. They live in an everlasting summer.

At some point during those years, Karl left the banking world for auditing work in private industry. Perhaps the pay was better for a man who now had a wife and two children to support. Towards the end of 1927, he accepted a job with a printing company called Friedrich Wilhelm Ruhfus, which claimed to be the world's oldest outdoor advertising company. It meant a move west to the city of Dortmund in the heart of the industrial Ruhr. Was it a great opportunity? Karl was to find himself in the wrong place at the wrong time.

3

Had they had the benefit of hindsight, the Niemanns would never have chosen to go to Dortmund. It was a dangerously unstable city in the late 1920s. They may have been drawn to Germany's second-biggest conurbation by the promise of a good salary for Karl in a solid printing company that dated back to 1866. They found a house in Dortmund-Brackel, a respectable neighbourhood on the east side. And there were outward signs of growing civic prosperity – Dortmund airport had opened in 1925, the same year as a giant concert complex, the Westfalenhalle. An enormous cinema, the Emelka, was one of five newly built, each one seating 2,000 customers.

Dortmund was the "city of smoke and soot", its skyline to the north a mass of chimneys. A powerhouse of the German economy, it was nevertheless vulnerable. Dortmund was over-dependent on heavy industry, with most of its workers employed in huge iron and steel works, industries that were the first to fall in any economic downturn, and the last to rise. The city had long since become a harbour for extremists on both right and left. In 1920, it was the heartland of the "Red Ruhr Army", when Communists fought paramilitaries of the right-wing Freikorps and dozens died. And it saw crippling hardship in the downturn of 1923–4, with half of the city occupied by the French, 78 coal mines shut down and 90% of its workers unemployed.

When the Niemanns moved there, the next abyss was still two years off. They had their own personal tragedy: in the spring of 1928, Minna's younger sister Irmgard, born when Minna was nearly fifteen, was knocked off her bike and killed on a Hameln bridge. For the rest of Minna's life, she had a picture of her dead sister hanging over her side of the bed.

Nothing suggests that the Niemanns were anything but a very unexceptional family during this period, Minna looking after their two children, Karl going to work. The political party that would eventually get his backing barely registered in the city. Fewer than one in a hundred Dortmunders voted for the Nazis in the 1928 elections. This was a left-leaning city, with the Social Democrats and Communists polling more than half the votes that year. In the wider world, the weak Weimar Republic was a shaky succession of coalitions that each lasted an average of eight months. But as long as the economy held together, nobody bothered too much.

Everything changed with the Wall Street crash of October 1929. The US called in German debts, industry collapsed and unemployment in the city rocketed in three years from 12,000 to 65,000. Karl continued to make his daily trek from the suburbs to his office close to the main railway station. But every time he entered the city centre, he stepped into a political cauldron. It was a fevered battleground for factions on the left and right. He may have found it frightening, intoxicating, even galvanising.

Nazis and other groups on the right churned out leaflet after leaflet, thrusting them into the hands of potential supporters, almost press-ganging ordinary citizens into taking up political affiliation. They slung up a huge banner on the city hall that read *Das Unglück*

Deutschlands sind die Juden (The Jews are Germany's downfall). The building was city-funded, but the authorities did not stop the banner being put up. Even many in left-leaning parties were rabidly anti-Semitic. Meanwhile, the Communists staged hunger marches through the streets, rounding up the unemployed and arming them with knuckle-dusters, knives and metal bars, so that they could scrap with the opposition.

The Nazis and smaller right-wing parties held their own marches. The left-wing *Westfälischer Kämpfer* newspaper caught some of the febrile atmosphere in a report published on 5th May 1930:

> *The main streets were cordoned off by the police to protect the Nazi bandits. The workers came again and again to the front, with the battle cry of the masses: "Death to fascism, Dortmund will stay Red, rule the streets."*

Karl's political baptism appears to have come in the late summer of 1930. In the Reichstag (parliament) elections of 14th September, the Nazis polled 24,934 votes in Dortmund. Even though it was a massive jump from only 1,965 votes two years before, it still represented only 8.3% of the city electorate. By comparison with the rest of the country, Dortmund was always a reluctant supporter of Hitler, lagging well behind in every election. Nationwide, the Nazis captured 6.4 million votes and catapulted 107 deputies into the Reichstag. The liberal *Tremonia* newspaper called it: "A catastrophic win for the National Socialists, consummate proof of the non-political sense of the German people."

The election result provided the trigger for Karl to act. He applied to join the Nazi Party two days later, although in most official records his party membership (number 415 176) was dated 1st January 1931. Almost immediately he volunteered for political office, signing up as the lowest-ranking official of the party, a *Blockwart* (block warden). His position was as a kind of recruiting sergeant for his district, knocking on doors, encouraging people to vote. Within a year, he had moved up one notch in the ranks to *Zellenwart* (cell leader), supervising between eight and ten block wardens.

Karl went to at least one political rally in that period, photographing a ragtag bunch of stormtroopers from the upstairs window of a building as they paraded through a communist district of the city. Hitler came to speak in the city twice – it is probable that Karl was among the mesmerised listeners. In the year 1931 alone, the Nazi Party held 470 political meetings in Dortmund. Discipline was tight and one would hazard a guess that Minna did not see much of her husband during that time.

What made Karl sign up for the swastika and do Hitler's work with enthusiasm? He did not become a member of the Nazi Party buoyed along by a tide of popular opinion. Even in the election that saw Hitler gain power in 1933, only a little more than a quarter of Dortmund's voters backed him. And in the printing company where he worked, Karl was the only party member.

Historians have emphasised the Nazi Party's ability to be all things to all men (and fewer women): the prospective voter cherry-picked the elements that chimed with their own aspirations. More importantly, it seemed to mine deep veins of dissatisfaction, readily finding scapegoats for Germany's post-war failings and offering a vague but alluring future based on nationalism and decisive action under a leader who was seen as powerful and charismatic. It was, as some have written, not so much a party as a movement, a dangerous appeal to the heart above the head.

Karl's son Rudi stated many times that his father had believed in Hitler: in many, if not all respects, Karl was predisposed to follow his Führer. An ex-soldier himself, just four years older than Karl, Hitler made a play for veterans of the Great War, creating a mythology about a *Dolchstoss*, a stab in the back that had seen Germany betrayed from within at the end of the war. Hitler portrayed the veterans as loyal patriots who deserved better. His exhortations must have found a receptive ear in Karl.

Other festering resentments that Hitler nursed might have resonated with Karl too. Hitler blamed the German surrender and economic woes on a deliberately undefined melange of "Jewish Bolsheviks". It is not difficult to imagine that a man who had spent a lifetime in banking and commerce would have been particularly troubled by the revolutionary fervour and destabilising influence of the Communist Party in overheated Dortmund. And it is highly improbable that Karl would have been anything but anti-Semitic, riding a wave of popular prejudice. Evidence from his later actions suggests just that.

The Nazi philosophy had a particular draw for the lower middle classes, whose lives had been blighted by the economic troughs of the 1920s. Clever propaganda portrayed a dynamic, decisive leader on a mission to save his country. Millions of Germans fell for it: Karl was one of them. And he was a comparatively early, willing volunteer at that.

In the Niemanns' adopted city, as in many other towns and cities throughout Germany, the route to totalitarianism during the first half of 1933 was not so much a path as a precipice. Dortmund academic Kurt Klotzbach noted that "hardly any sector of the political, social and economic life of the city was spared". The swastika was raised over the city hall two days after the Nazis gained 43% of the vote nationwide in the Reichstag election in March. The main streets were renamed within the week. Rathenau-Allee became Adolf-Hitler-Allee, Stresemannstrasse became Göringstrasse and what had been Republikplatz was named Horst Wessel-Platz, after the young Nazi "martyr" who wrote the lyrics to the Nazi's turgid national anthem.

At the end of March, stormtroopers barged into the offices of each of the liberal and left-leaning newspapers and made them change their editorial stance, or closed them down. Stormtrooper thugs stood at the entrances of every Jewish shop on 1st April to enforce a boycott of Jewish businesses and more than 200 leading Jews were imprisoned. The "maladjusted" and "non-Aryans" in higher administrative roles were removed from office that spring.

Karl and Minna's own children very quickly felt the insinuation of Nazism into their young lives. Seven-year-old Dieter would not have remembered a time before Hitler. The little boy's storybooks portrayed Hitler as a benevolent father figure. Dieter was made to recite: "I will always obey you as I obey my father and mother."

Anne was nine years old when Hitler came to power. Every day, she went into a classroom where a picture of Hitler hung on the wall. Her teacher greeted the class with "Heil Hitler!" at the start of the lesson, and the children returned a "Heil Hitler!" at the end. If any child did not respond in this manner, they would be disciplined. A government directive made sure that every subject was transformed to fall into line with "the spirit of National Socialism". Biology emphasised the role of racial purity, history taught about the supremacy of Germanic peoples and the degeneracy of Jews. Politically unacceptable teachers were weeded out: by 1936, 97% of teachers had conformed to the regime by becoming members of the National Socialist Teachers' League.

In November that year, on her tenth birthday, Anne joined a club, the Jungmädel, the Young Girls' League. It was the junior section of the girls' equivalent to the Hitler Youth. It was the only club left open to girls by that time and attendance was compulsory.

Karl was expected to play his part in tightening the noose on his fellow citizens. His Nazi Party position was renamed *Stellenleiter*. It was more than just a change of title. He was now under orders to supervise his team of *Blockleiters* in spying on the local populace, doorstepping them to instruct them on Nazi doctrine and ensuring that anyone who was politically suspect was reported to "the relevant authorities": that is to say, the Gestapo. That was the theory; in practice these lowly officials often had little influence. Before, and during the war, Karl was willing to show his full pedigree and listed "*Stellenleiter*" on official forms. In compulsory questionnaires filled in after the war, when the onus was on citizens to downplay their involvement and commitment to Nazism, Karl omitted to mention his marginally more senior post and simply wrote "*Blockleiter*".

In May 1933, during a period when all other political parties were abolished, the trade unions were dissolved. They were replaced by a single body; the Deutsche Arbeitsfront (DAF), a Nazi-run organisation that purported to represent all workers. It would – so they claimed – put an end to all class conflict by cultivating *Volksgemeinschaft* (the people's community) and "joy in work". It would end "the malicious exploitation of labour power". Karl volunteered to act as shop steward for the DAF at his own place of work.

His new "union" role proved to be the beginning of the end for Karl at Friedrich Wilhelm Ruhfus, the printing company where he had worked since 1927. Fired up by his new responsibilities, Karl insisted that the company should pay the workers a tariff, one that had long since fallen into abeyance. Faced with the probability of official retribution should he refuse, Herr Lehmann, Karl's manager, felt he had no alternative but to agree to Karl's demands. Their relationship deteriorated over this and a number of other issues and, eventually, Karl was sacked.

It was a bad time to be thrown out of work. Minna had given birth in March 1934 to their third child, Rudolf (Rudi). Karl was thrown a lifeline – a job with the DAF as a local group treasurer. But his salary had now fallen from 6,000 to 2,600 marks. It was, in effect, little more than an honorarium. By the middle of 1935, the man with a wife and three children to support was in a parlous financial situation.

Chance played a role in Karl's next, fateful move. The Niemanns shared their house with the family of their landlord, one Adolf Opitz. The Niemanns lived on one floor, the Opitz family on the other. The two families were certainly friends – good enough friends that their children played together, and amateur beekeeper Opitz was made one of baby Rudi's patrons. The child was christened with Adolf as one of his middle names. Karl talked to Herr Opitz about his predicament and his landlord offered to intercede on his behalf with an acquaintance, a senior official in the government.

Opitz's contact was very senior indeed. August Heissmeyer was at that time head of the SS Main Office. He was Heinrich Himmler's deputy, a man who wielded considerable clout. There was a good reason why Heissmeyer might be predisposed to favour Karl – Heissmeyer had gone to the same school in Hameln, though he was nearly three years younger so it is unlikely that they were actually friends. Opitz arranged for the two men to meet. Karl must have impressed: in no time, Heissmeyer pulled strings. He contacted another very important Nazi, an SS administrative leader based in the south called Obergruppenführer Oswald Pohl. It was Pohl who found Karl a job. It would mean a doubling of Karl's salary and a move to a location just outside Munich. Karl would go on ahead, settle into his new post and find accommodation for the family. In October 1935, he boarded a train to Bavaria.

Dear Lord, Make Me Dumb

4

It is much like any other picturesque town in Bavaria. Pretty, winding streets, colourful buildings on either side with shuttered windows, some with stepped roofs. A fountain in the marketplace. An onion-shaped dome on top of the church. From the top of the hill, you can look out on a clear day to the snow-capped peaks of the Alps.

Artists flocked to the town in the nineteenth century. It was said that a painter lived in every tenth house. They came to draw the countryside below, a wild, romantic landscape of reeds, fens and big skies. But by the time the First World War broke out, much of the marshland had been drained. On one of those reclaimed areas outside the town, a gunpowder and munitions factory was built, to fuel the distant slaughter.

Today, few visitors come to explore the beautiful heart of this town. Those who do make it through the doors of the tourist information office are given a free white pencil with a message printed on it that speaks volumes about the town's efforts to change perceptions: *Dachau – Viel mehr Stadt als Sie denken* (Dachau – Much more to the town than you think). However, when I spoke to a young Berliner in London, he gave the more widely held view:

"Dachau is a word that eats into the heart of every German."

On an autumn day in 1935, Karl left Dachau railway station and headed through open fields towards the concentration camp, to begin his new job. Newspapers in Dortmund would have given him a slanted picture of the concentration camp's purpose and character. They portrayed it as a kind of house of correction for those who disturbed the state – the "rabble rousers", "grumblers" and "work-shy". Political troublemakers were supposedly taken into "protective custody" to be transformed into decent citizens through strict discipline and re-education.

It was known that prisoners had died "trying to escape". There had been a court case – it had collapsed. Locals suspected some of what was going on. One of them was jailed for looking into the camp. Many thought it was best to let things be.

At the time when Karl arrived, the future of Dachau concentration camp – and indeed of all concentration camps – appeared to be in doubt. After a wave of initial arrests when Hitler came to power, most prisoners had been released. There were not many more than a thousand inmates in the concrete barrack huts of Dachau – buildings left over from the old munitions factory – and around 4,500 in total throughout Germany. The minister for the interior complained to the Führer about the cost of running the camps.

Karl did not go to work at the concentration camp itself, but within a much bigger complex next door that included the camp guards' barracks and a garrison for a new military wing of the SS (the Schutzstaffel – literally "protective squadrons"), that would eventually become known as the Waffen SS. Karl was taking up the post of auditor for an SS training camp on the site, which had opened just a few weeks before.

The new recruit suddenly found himself elevated to a position of some status. While Oswald Pohl ran the SS administration from offices in Munich, he lived in Dachau itself, and very frequently visited the training camp on Sundays. Pohl valued his auditors to a high degree: he had been a navy paymaster himself during the Great War and understood the influence that those who inspected the books could wield. It is not unreasonable to think that Pohl would have seen a great deal of Karl during those first few months and that Karl would have felt a lift in self-esteem, as the under-appreciated years in poorly paid jobs facing suspicion and open hostility fell away behind him.

With the job came membership of the SS. Karl was entering a paramilitary organisation, putting on a dazzling black uniform like all his new comrades, decorating it with the pride of his youth – his Iron Cross (First Class), the ribbons of the Cross of Honour. He regained an officer's rank – he was SS-Scharführer (troop leader) Karl Niemann. It was made clear to him, repeatedly, that he was entering an élite. He was told "an SS man brings more discipline and the dedication which is an absolute must for this work. More can be demanded of him than from a civilian. He is more worthy…" Karl gave his oath:

I swear to you, Adolf Hitler, as Führer and Chancellor of the Reich, loyalty and bravery. I pledge to you, and to the superiors you have selected, obedience until death, so help me God.

Over the next seven months, Karl lived and breathed the SS. Isolated from his family and friends and even townspeople who might dare to voice a dissenting opinion – for he probably took accommodation within the barracks – Karl underwent a process of radicalisation. It started with an induction into the SS. The training camp was at the core of Nazi ideology. He began a six-week course held, according to fellow officer Jürgen Stroop, "in complete isolation and a monastic-like atmosphere". Stroop explained:

> *The lectures and seminars covered, among other things, Hitler's biography, National Socialist doctrine, an extensive course on the history of the (Nazi Party), and race theory... The Officer-Cadet Training School also gave us administrative training. We practised spelling, sentence construction, grammar, learned specific terminology, correspondence, business management of SS firms etc. But above all, it was about party discipline.*

That same officer spoke of a marvellous "fraternal spirit". It was a comradeship that embraced anti-Semitism, racism of all kinds and a hatred of those who opposed the regime. And though a wire fence separated the training camp from the concentration camp, there was no barrier between the trainee officers and those officers already working in the camp. It was fully expected that Karl should socialise in the SS *Gemeinschaftshaus*, the SS community building.

Dachau was not a big operation at that time. Karl would have known every one of his fellow officers personally. He would have rubbed shoulders and drunk beer with Rudolf Höss, a man who had beaten a schoolteacher to death and would go on to order the killing of more than a million Jews as *Kommandant* of Auschwitz. He would have chatted with Max Kögel, who later had gas chambers installed at Majdanek in Poland; Hans Loritz, *Kommandant* of Dachau and Sachsenhausen, who took special pleasure from torturing Jews; Franz Trenkle, deputy officer at both Dachau and Bergen-Belsen, who confessed to shooting helpless prisoners; Martin Weiss, later *Kommandant* of Neuengamme, Dachau and Majdanek. These were murderers, psychotics, fanatics. Karl was drinking at a very poisonous trough.

As part of his induction, he may have spent some time as a guard within the concentration camp. Like the officers who would go on to run the most notorious concentration camps, the SS guards had been trained in the "Dachau school". Their teacher had been Theodor Eicke, a *Kommandant* who had been promoted to inspector of all camps as his reward for killing Hitler's stormtrooper leader (and emerging rival) Ernst Röhm during the Night of the Long Knives the year before. Eicke had laid down rules for running the camp:

> *Tolerance is weakness. Knowing this, we will act ruthlessly wherever we must to defend the Fatherland. Our decent fellow citizens will not be affected by these regulations. But let any political agitators and intellectual subversives, whatever their leanings, pay heed: take care that you are not caught or you will be seized by the throat and silenced using your own methods.*

Auschwitz *Kommandant* Rudolf Höss gave a vivid insight into the particular attitude of mind of camp staff:

> *Eicke's intention was to lay a foundation of hostility in his SS men towards the prisoners, to stir them up against them, to repress any flicker of sympathy. He did this through constant lectures on the criminality and dangerous nature of the prisoners and corresponding orders. His unceasing efforts in this vein aroused a virulent hatred, an antipathy towards the prisoners, especially in the cruder men, that is beyond the imagination of outsiders. This attitude spread to all SS men and officers posted in concentration camps.*
>
> *Any trace of sympathy gives the "enemies of the state" an opening they will exploit immediately. Pity for "enemies of the state" is unworthy of an SS man. Weaklings have no place in his ranks and would be well advised to withdraw to a monastery as quickly as*

possible. He could only use hard, determined men who obeyed every order unflinchingly. They did not wear the Totenkopf (death's head) emblem for nothing and it was no coincidence that their weapons were always loaded. They were the only soldiers who guarded the enemy even during peacetime, day and night, the enemy behind barbed wire.

5

When Karl left for Dachau, Minna did not hang about in Dortmund. As a cost-saving measure, she took the children to stay at her mother's home in Hameln. One story of their time there survives and it came to light in 1990, when Anne paid a return visit to the town of her birth.

On a hot summer's afternoon, Anne stood outside her old house in Adolfstrasse with her sixteen-year-old granddaughter Kirsten. She had taken the girl with her on her annual three-week holiday to Germany, staying, as always, with her youngest brother, Ekart. That day, they were going on a trip down memory *strasse*.

Kirsten recalled that it was not a happy experience for her grandmother. As they walked from house to house, Anne talked about the people she had known who lived there. They stopped outside one building and Anne broke down in tears. When she recovered herself, she told Kirsten that it had belonged to the family of a good friend from school, and that she had visited there many times and met her family. The good friend was Jewish. Anne added that she had had other Jewish friends in that father-free spell in Hameln. But word of Anne's doings had reached Karl in Bavaria and an order came back – Anne was not to speak to any Jews. A short while later, the friend she had been told to shun did not turn up at school. Somebody went to the house and found it empty: the family had simply disappeared and was never heard of again.

While Minna and the children waited in Hameln, a postcard arrived in February 1936 from the Winter Olympics in Garmisch-Partenkirchen. Karl was attending – most likely in an official capacity. Did he see the skiers? Did he watch the bobsleigh? Had he seen the Führer? Karl's message was succinct: "Greetings – with love from Daddy."

It was not until June 1936, when Karl was thoroughly settled into his job, that he found a house for his family. By the time Minna arrived in Dachau with the children, Karl was wearing a different uniform to the one she knew – he was the man in black with SS runes on his lapel. Anne was by now a teenager, with her hair plaited in the classic Aryan *mädchen* style of the period. Ten-year-old Dieter had already begun his obligatory attendance in the Deutsches Jungvolk, the junior section of the Hitler Youth. Toddler Rudi was learning his first words. Instead of "Mutti" he could say only "Hu-te-te".

The family moved into a large detached modern house beneath the castle, as tenants of a staunch Catholic called Martin Weinsteiger. The two families appeared to get on well – the children played together.

Both tenant and landlord underwent a test of friendship and fanaticism when a Jesuit priest was arrested in Munich and sent to the concentration camp. Weinsteiger objected, launching a very public campaign to have the cleric released. This was a dangerous thing to do. Weinsteiger knew – everybody knew – the doggerel verse that typified local attitudes and fears about the camp:

Lieber Gott, mach mich dumm,
dass ich nicht nach Dachau kumm.

Dear Lord, make me dumb,
that I may not to Dachau come.

Weinsteiger must have been aware that Karl could – and strictly speaking should – have denounced his friend to the authorities. But Karl said nothing.

Whether Minna had seen changes in her husband in the Dachau years is simply not known. What is known is that on public holidays she accompanied him on office outings. The SS officers and their wives piled into cars and headed for the Alps. On Hitler's birthday, they strolled through the town of Mittenwald, its streets bedecked with swastikas, hanging from windows in public displays of compulsory loyalty. The SS group walked in the mountains and drank in taverns, the men embracing Bavarian customs by wearing lederhosen. Little Rudi was taken on at least one of these trips. Minna dutifully smiled for the camera.

In the summer of 1937, at the age of 42, Minna was pregnant with her fourth child. It was a difficult pregnancy for a comparatively old mother-to-be with heart problems. Karl had difficulties in his own head. Nearly all citizens of the Reich belonged to either the Catholic or Protestant Church. Nazi ideologues disapproved of both. The Catholics were governed from Rome, and both churches studied the Old Testament with its stories of "degenerate Jews". The churches taught compassion for the weak – a concept fundamentally at odds with the Nazi emphasis on survival of the fittest.

A movement called *Kirchenaustritt* (Church Exit) had begun in the party, calling for members to break from the established churches. While the general population largely shunned it, the SS supported it to a large extent and a quarter of its members abandoned their established religion. Karl was one of them. He cited personal differences when he left the Lutheran Church in October 1937, and, like the others, classified himself thereafter as *gottgläubig*, a believer in God.

The SS chief Heinrich Himmler drove this anti-Christian, neo-pagan movement, which urged devotees to downgrade Christmas in favour of celebrating the winter solstice. The replacement for a nativity scene in the family home was meant to be a clay pot, a candle holder decorated with traditional Germanic six-spoked runic wheels. It was known as a *Julleuchter* (Yule lantern). Himmler explained its purpose: "I would have every family of a married SS man to be in possession of a *Julleuchter*. Even the wife will, when she has left the myths of the Church, find something else which her heart and mind can embrace." Every year, a candle was sent to the Niemann house to be placed and lit on top of this lumpy article of faith. Every year, Minna made a point of religiously tossing it straight into the bin.

Minna quite deliberately left Dachau in February 1938 to have her baby. Ekart (Eki) was born in neighbouring Prittlbach. His mother did not want her son's birth certificate besmirched with the name of Dachau. The child was given the middle name of Josef, after Karl's baby-faced superior officer Sturmbannführer Josef Spacil.* A year later, Minna would be rewarded for her fecundity in producing four Aryan children for the Reich by being given the *Mutterkreuz* (the Mother's Cross). It granted special privileges to holders, and members of the Hitler Youth were under orders to salute any mother wearing such a decoration. "Did she wear it?" "Pah!" snorted Eki. "She threw it away."

While Minna nursed her infant, Karl played with the baby's older brother. One of Rudi's first memories was of being bounced on his father's knee, while his father sang the song that Rudi himself would in turn sing to his niece, sons and grandson.

Hoppe hoppe Reiter
Wenn er fällt, dann schreit er,
Fällt er in den Graben,
Fressen ihn die Raben.
Fällt er in den Sumpf,
Dann macht der Reiter... plumpfs!

Bumpety bumpety, rider,
If he falls, then he cries

---

* Spacil was an especially cunning and devious character. Alleged (but never proved) to be involved in circulating forged British banknotes to buy items on the black market, this economist's greatest notoriety came in the dying days of the regime, when he emptied the Berlin Reichsbank of 23 million marks-worth of looted gold and foreign currency at gunpoint and had it hidden in the Alps. Nobody knows whether he surrendered it all to the Americans. After the war, shady Spacil avoided trial and punishment.

If he falls into the ditch,
The ravens will eat him.
If he falls into the swamp,
Then the rider goes... splash!

The family's house in Burgfriedenstrasse 31 was about two miles from the training camp. By now, the concentration camp had filled and taken on more staff. The authorities put on public transport. Karl was able to catch the 7.02am bus to work.

6

Pigs and chickens gave Karl his big break. The lowly auditor and troop leader had been underemployed in general financial administration and so he began to accumulate new responsibilities. Pig pens and poultry houses were built within the training camp in 1936 and Karl was given charge of a handful of civilians, who in turn controlled the work of about twenty concentration camp inmates who were pulled in from next door. With that, his job began to morph into that of a business manager. He worked under Gerhard Maurer, one-time accountant, travel agent, dabbler in banking, publisher.

The camp administrators, who employed inmates to push a heavy roller around for no reason other than to punish them and for the gratification of sadistic guards, were beginning to see the economic potential of labour. Initially it was a drive for self-sufficiency. A bakery fulfilled the camp needs. Workshop huts were built to use skilled workers from among the inmates in butchery, plumbing, shoemaking, clothing repair and manufacture, and carpentry. In time, there would be a porcelain factory in the complex. Karl may have had a role in its financial management – he certainly took home plenty of china figures mounted on horseback to display around his house – Frederick the Great, a Prussian Hussar, a general or two.

In September 1936, Hitler announced a four-year plan to put Germany on a military and economic war footing. Labour was now short: all hands to the pumps. Dachau responded. A building project outside the camp housed an expanding workforce. Within the camp, prisoners began to level the ground and build new wooden barrack huts. The new Kommandant, Hans Loritz, took cruelty to new levels. Karl could look through the fence or step upstairs and look down over the camp at any time. He had every opportunity to see what was going on inside.

Inmate Alfred Hübsch recalled:

The year 1937 was a horribly hard year for us Dachauers. That is when construction of the new large camp, soon notorious throughout the whole world, began. 4 o'clock wake up, 5.30 line-up for roll-call, 6 o'clock work began. At six in the evening work was over and roll-call followed again. The penal company then had to work even longer, until dark. Work the whole day without a break, workdays, Sundays and holidays; it made no difference at all. Until May 1938 there was not a single day off in Dachau with the exception of Christmas Day.

Another inmate spoke of having to carry concrete on his bare shoulders in baking sun. Men were ordered to run rather than walk. Those who fell short in the new regime were whipped or beaten in front of their fellow inmates.

The frenetic pace of activity within the camp was matched (though rather more humanely) in the training camp complex, where luckier inmates were brought to work. Inmate Ludwig Schecher said: "Carpentry quickly became a big business, with the mass production of bedsteads, lockers, tables and stools made for the establishment of concentration camps and barracks." Six hundred inmates worked with wood and Karl took on management of the prison enterprise, placing orders for timber and supervising quality control.

The inmates – nearly all non-Jewish German men at this time – were working to equip new camps. Buchenwald, Flossenbürg, Mauthausen and Sachsenhausen all opened between 1936 and 1938. The camps were deliberately sited next to quarries or clay pits, so that the free labour would provide the bricks and stone to satisfy Hitler's dreams for giant buildings in a rebuilt capital city. A government edict in late 1937 had provided a quick excuse for the arrest and imprisonment of 12,000 "work-shy" and "asocial" people, including homosexuals and Jehovah's Witnesses. In 1938, Dachau's prison population swelled to 11,000.

Dachau pioneered the use of slave labour. But management was chaotic and sometimes corrupt. Nominally under the control of the training camp, the SS enterprises were also governed to some extent by the SS office in Munich, causing great inefficiency. Not only that, testimony from inmate Schecher pointed to a prevalence in the camp of what he called "bungling – the illegal fulfilment of the illicit desires of the SS camp leaders, from the camp *Kommandant* right down to the lowliest troop leader".

From the government's point of view, it was one thing to beat up and murder inmates, but for camp staff to use inmate labour for their own ends, making money at the expense of the state – that was just unacceptable. The Nazi leadership took steps to end the corruption and inefficiency.

They turned to the man who had given Karl his break at Dachau in the first place. SS administrative supremo Obergruppenführer Oswald Pohl was empire-building and now turned his attention to SS industries. A power struggle ensued with Theodor Eicke, former

Dachau *Kommandant* and now overall manager of the concentration camps. Pohl won. Himmler gave him administrative charge of SS enterprises in all concentration camps. Pohl decided to centralise the whole operation from Berlin. Karl was told he was being transferred to the capital.

In the Dachau years, Karl had risen up the hierarchy. By his own admission, he was, by the end, working at times directly for Obergruppenführer Pohl. SS Untersturmführer Niemann (second lieutenant) was now a middle-ranking officer. His first promotions from lowly troop leader had occurred automatically every year on Hitler's birthday. But this commissioned officer rank had had to be earned. In order to qualify, Karl had to submit a *Lebenslauf*, a CV of his career to date, listing his achievements. He received a testing letter from the SS Race and Settlement Office wanting proof of racial pedigree. They demanded physical inspections by a doctor of his wife and children "information about external appearance (size, weight, skin, hair, eye colour and similar)". The family must have passed their trial of racial purity. Karl gained his commission and it was signed by Heinrich Himmler. At an official ceremony, he was presented with an SS sword.

In June 1938, Karl left for Berlin. For the second time in three years, Minna went back to Hameln with the children and waited to be summoned.

Berlin

7

On Wednesday 15th June 1938, SS-Untersturmführer Karl Niemann stepped off a train in Germany's capital and went to temporary lodgings in Augsburgerstrasse, just off Kurfürstendamm, in the heart of the city.

We do not know exactly when Minna and the children went to join him in Berlin. If the family had still been in Hameln on the night of 9th November, they would have seen the flames from the town's burning synagogue. On the infamous *Kristallnacht*, the president of the Jewish community was dragged out of his house to see the building destroyed, then taken to Buchenwald concentration camp and murdered.

If the family were with Karl in Berlin by that date, they would have heard about – if not witnessed – similar scenes. The *Daily Telegraph* correspondent noted:

Mob law ruled in Berlin throughout the afternoon and evening and hordes of hooligans indulged in an orgy of destruction... Racial hatred and hysteria seemed to have taken complete hold of otherwise decent people. I saw fashionably dressed women clapping their hands and screaming with glee, while respectable middle-class mothers held up their babies to see the "fun".

The "fun" was shop windows being smashed, Jewish people being beaten up and humiliated and synagogues set on fire. Karl could have read in *Das Schwarze Korps*, the SS house journal, two weeks later:

> *The German people are not in the least inclined to tolerate in their country hundreds of thousands of criminals, who not only secure their existence through crime, but also want to exact revenge... These hundreds of thousands of Jews [would establish] a breeding ground for Bolshevism and a collection of the politically criminal subhuman elements... In such a situation we would be faced with the hard necessity of exterminating the Jewish underworld in the same way as, under our government of law and order, we are accustomed to exterminating any other criminals – that is by fire and sword. The result would be the actual and final end of Jewry in Germany, its absolute annihilation.*

Such unpleasantness was most likely far from the minds of Karl's family. They were moving into a purpose-built SS housing estate, an idyllic location right at the end of the underground line, on the edge of the Grunewald forest, and close to the pretty bow-shaped Krumme Lanke lake. The so-called SS *Kameradschaftssiedlung* (camaraderie settlement) in Berlin-Zehlendorf was the fulfilment of a goal set by Reichsführer Heinrich Himmler, who had desired "a closed community for the officers of the SS". The estate architect promised: "The tenants' souls will be filled with true comradeship. Divisions among them by fences will be superfluous. They will take up residence in a beautiful spirit of comradeship under the treetops of the local pines."

It was (and still is) a beautiful location. The houses had a rustic appearance, scattered among standing pines, the steep roofs clad in beaver-tail-shaped tiles, the windows shuttered, the house fronts given a half-timbered look.

SS officers were given the chance to name the roads in which they lived and, not surprisingly, they selected names that accorded with Nazi ideology. The two main roads were named after dead heroes of the Reich. The naming of the side streets became the subject of a prize competition in the SS newsletter *Das Schwarze Korps. Im Kinderland* (In the land of children) came at the suggestion of an SS officer's wife, who said: "The men, who represent the racial elite of the German people, pass on their high-quality genetic material to a large number of genetically wealthy offspring." The 21 families in Karl's street agreed on Dienstweg (Service Way). The size of the house allocated depended on rank. Karl was given one of the estate's terraced houses, for which he paid 105 marks a month. High-ranking officers were detached in more ways than one.

Although the house was – to modern eyes – comparatively small for a family of six, the Niemanns were thrilled to have a home all to themselves at last. The estate was full of toddlers and small children playing together in box sandpits in communal garden spaces. The adults had bird boxes put up in all of the pine trees. The Niemann grown-ups held a party for their neighbours on New Year's Day 1939. This was a new life, a new beginning away from tainted Dachau.

The children knew that their father was an important man now. Every day, he dressed in a military uniform for work – jodhpurs, peaked cap, Iron Cross pinned to his breast pocket. Every day, a car would draw up in the road outside and a chauffeur would drive him off to a big job somewhere in the big city. And when he came back at night, he would often potter about in the garden absent-mindedly, tending his kohlrabi root vegetables, staking the redcurrants, nursing seedlings in his cold frame, sometimes still dressed in his uniform.

8

The office secretary was given a tiny job that was intended to promote joviality and mutual backslapping among her bosses, a mundane oiling of the wheels of corporate culture. She typed out a birthday list for the senior managers. Additional niceties were duly observed; the big boss's wife was included, although the date of her birth was omitted – one does not tell a lady's age. December 24th was reserved for the *Christkind*, the Christ child. There was evidently a level of joshing and informality among senior staff of the SS, for several managers' names were prefaced with nicknames. Richard Bauer, for example, was dubbed "Ritzipitzi". One wonders whether the men and women he worked to death or gassed, called the Auschwitz *Kommandant* "Ritzipitzi".

This was life inside the organisation which became known as the Wirtschaftsverwaltungshauptamt (WVHA), the SS Business and Administration Main Office. At Nuremberg, eighteen of its leaders were to stand in the dock to hear the opening statement:

The crimes which are the subject of this trial run the gamut of "man's inhumanity to man" – the systematic commission of atrocities in concentration camps, the utilisation of slave labour under brutal and inhumane conditions, the extermination of the Jews and so-called "useless eaters", criminal medical experimentation on concentration camp inmates, the destruction of the Warsaw ghetto, and the confiscation of property on a gigantic scale. The defendant Pohl and his collaborators in the WVHA were parties to all of these crimes and many more.

For seven years, Karl worked within the WVHA. He never made it on to the birthday list. Though he would rank among the hundred most senior staff in an empire that eventually swelled to employ 1,500 in its Berlin offices, and was himself promoted to *SS-Hauptsturmführer* (equivalent to a British army captain), he never rose above middle management. Whether it was down to lack of ambition, ability, or sheer luck, Karl was always the deputy, never the chief.

His career at the WVHA began and ended with wood. The technical knowledge he had gained from managing the workshops at Dachau evidently equipped him to run woodworking enterprises within all of the concentration camps. By 1939, this work had been subsumed within an SS company called the Deutsche Ausrüstungswerke (DAW), the German Equipment Works. It started small – there were no more than a dozen staff when war broke out. Nothing changed when hostilities commenced, but SS industries mushroomed as the Wehrmacht overran country after country and hundreds of thousands of civilians were put behind barbed wire. By 1941, nearly two-thirds of its slave labourers were in occupied Poland. These were, as one historian drily observed, the economics of misery.

Karl was a fixed point in an industrial concern that, in this growing phase, reorganised and restructured just about every year. The SS business enterprises operated out of a row of high-rise offices on Unter den Eichen* in Lichterfelde, a district south of Berlin's city centre. An offshoot near Sachsenhausen in the north of the city managed the concentration camps. There were strong links within the organisation, which was run on military lines, with all its officers dressed for work in military uniform. In some offices, wholly staffed by former soldiers or policemen, the staff addressed each other by rank rather than by name. The overall boss, Oswald Pohl, demanded that his staff should be "office soldiers with a military bearing". The WVHA observed a strict hierarchy and a stifling bureaucracy.

Profit was secondary to ideological zeal. Nazi doctrines were spouted by the senior managers to all their staff, of course, but it would appear that it coursed through the veins of middle managers such as Karl too. An officer of equivalent rank left a "memo to self" that gives an illuminating glimpse into the prevailing ethics:

> *The business undertakings of the Schutzstaffel [SS] are the best means to breathe new life into National Socialist ideals, to let them become reality, to blaze new trails in the area of applied socialism. We must live socialism as the deed! Our example must spur other corporations forward to emulate us in order to see the growth of a healthy, satisfied and happy* Volk.†

Just as American settlers went west without giving any consideration to the native Americans, the WVHA was driven by the desire to create what they referred to as a "New Order" of pure German communities in the conquered lands to the east. New buildings

---

* Translates as Under the Oaks. The most famous Berlin street is Unter den Linden (under the limes).
† The People

would need furnishing. Karl was registered as a manager in two furniture-making companies within occupied Czechoslovakia. He signed a statement to confirm his suitability:

I, SS-Hauptsturmführer Karl Niemann... hereby declare under penalty of perjury that I am not a Jew for the purposes of the provisions of item 6 of the Regulations of the Reich Protector in Bohemia and Moravia.

In time, furnishing the peace would become secondary to saving the war. Dinner tables for settlers would be sacrificed for making window frames and doors for bomb-damaged houses. But that was all unthinkable in those first years of euphoric and unbridled expansion.

How many of Karl's work colleagues, bonded by ideological certainties, became his friends? One name, and one name only, slipped out of the SS headquarters and into the family home in Dienstweg 19. Both elderly Niemann brothers gave a flicker of recognition at the mention of Karl Bestle: "Yes, I remember that name," said Eki. Neither son recalled anything about Munich-born Bestle. Perhaps his name was bandied about at home, perhaps Bestle even visited Dienstweg. But the two Karls' working lives were intertwined and there is a little circumstantial evidence that their association continued long after the war.

Bestle was an architect by profession, a Nazi by conviction. At just seventeen years of age he was involved in Hitler's infamous Munich Putsch of 1923, when a rabble of paramilitaries tried to seize power in a brief but bloody revolt. In the early years of the regime, Bestle battled with the authorities to be recognised with the *Blutorden*, the coveted Blood Order award given to those who had been there. When the post-war reckoning came, Bestle made light of his part, claiming that his unit of junior soldiers had been sent into an officer college, where they stayed awaiting further orders for two days, by which time it was all over. The story sounds so ludicrous, it might even be true.

Nevertheless Bestle's record shows a long and high level of political commitment. He was fined for wearing a Nazi cockade when the organisation was banned after the Putsch. He was in the extreme right-wing Bavarian Freikorps, various nationalist groups and, for a year, the stormtroopers. In Munich, the unemployed architect joined the police and spent a few months within the force as a guard at Dachau. When the police moved out, Bestle moved in, leaving the force to become a financial administrator in the training camp. He would have known and worked closely with Karl Niemann in those years. Like Karl, he was transferred to Berlin.

Another individual brought up from Dachau and known to Karl was Gerhard Maurer, his old boss at the SS training camp. He remained in charge of the Berlin office until a transfer of power ended in a very nasty case of office politics.

In September 1941, Maurer was replaced as Karl's manager by a 31-year-old who was parachuted into Berlin out of nowhere. Dr Kurt May was the son and successor of a well-known Stuttgart furniture manufacturer. He was a shrewd and ambitious businessman, who had bought out the Jewish owners of companies in occupied Czech lands at the start of the war. Similar attempts by the SS to set up industrial concerns had been consistently blocked by the man in charge of this territory, Konstantin von Neurath, an old-school aristocrat and former foreign minister who had managed to survive the Nazi purges by being shunted by Hitler into the Czech backwaters as the *Reichsprotektor*. Von Neurath was committed to defying the SS at every turn.

Dr May was courted by SS boss Oswald Pohl, who saw an opportunity for subterfuge. The two men met up. They agreed a deal whereby May was appointed head of the SS office in charge of woodworking industries where Karl worked, and his factories were subsumed under the aegis of the SS within a new company, the German Noble Furniture Company. Thus the SS took control under a cloak of private enterprise and Neurath's resistance was overcome.

For a while, the new concern thrived, boosted by the installation of new machinery. May had a driving enthusiasm for producing low-cost quality furniture for ordinary Germans, an IKEA for the Nazis. He even had a showroom to display his wares in Berlin's exclusive Potsdammerstrasse. Then, in January 1942, a fire burned down one of the factories. Arson was suspected and the Criminal Police became involved.

They began to focus, not on the cause of the fire, which appeared to be an accident, but on May's dealings in obtaining the factory. A senior SS officer warned darkly that "the good Dr May could not be helped any more". The police discovered that May had bought the factory from a Jewish entrepreneur called Drucker and had arranged the necessary paperwork for the former owner to emigrate to New Zealand. The purchase was normal business practice in 1940 when the transaction was negotiated, but "being soft on Jews" and enabling one to escape was viewed in a very different light by 1942.

May found himself isolated, shut out by an office of close colleagues. He lacked friends in high places too. Pohl proved to be no ally, turning on the man he now saw as a betrayer of Nazi ideals. In July, May was arrested and imprisoned by the Gestapo. He was stripped of his position in the same month. Karl gained yet another new manager in the shape of Josef Opperbeck, already a seasoned senior figure within the WVHA. In April 1943, after nine months in Gestapo captivity, May was released. By then, the SS had wrested the Czech enterprises from his control.*

Karl, well connected, secure in his own position, was able to trumpet in a statement that spring:

> *The main task of the corporation is, first of all, to weed out all Jewish traces of the operation. And through the installation of new, modern machines as well as through the restoration of the buildings to working order, the corporation must be reorganised in such a way that corresponds to all the demands of the current time.*

---

* Kurt May had, to say the least, a chequered career thereafter. He occupied a variety of roles before he was dismissed by Himmler from the SS in September 1944. May ended the war fighting on the Russian front. His furniture company went into liquidation and he disappeared from view, surfacing in bizarre circumstances in 1962 to give evidence in the Frankfurt trial of the Auschwitz *Kommandant's* adjutant, Robert Mulka. When May testified that he had been overall manager of the company that made doors for the gas chambers, suspicion at once fell upon him. But May, sensing trouble, fled abroad. He died in 1978 having never been brought to trial.

9

Rudi Niemann was just a small child when he first saw the strangers come into his house. They said nothing to him. The men – and they were always men – entered Dienstweg 19 many times. Rudi was struck most of all by their uniform, the like of which he had never seen before: "They had a big, kind of greyish horrible-looking dress, with, at the back, 'Jude'."

These men in striped pyjamas, whose coarse cloth revolted the little boy, were brought from Sachsenhausen concentration camp and possibly its sub-camps too. The SS had its own private supply of workers, a perk of the job, and Karl made use of them, even during the war years, when most people in Berlin had virtually no access to plumbers, electricians, carpenters and other tradesmen, since they had been drafted to the front. Carpenters from the camp brought over the furniture they had made to order in the workshop; quality, well-carved items made of oak by skilled men The men in stripes carried a bookcase over the threshold, a round table and heavy chairs with bowed legs, and a huge cupboard, all to furnish the family's new suburban home.

The concentration camp inmates who came into the house never spoke to Rudi and the boy had been carefully taught not to speak to them either: "Because, see, they were really, ah, non-Aryans, so therefore you didn't mix with them. And they were grown-ups. You didn't talk to them either." The social taboo regarding speaking to Jews was reinforced for Rudi by the official rules, which dictated that civilians were prohibited from speaking to the prisoners who came to their homes.

One person in the house flouted the rules behind closed doors. Rudi's mother not only spoke freely to the inmates, she made them *Kaffee und Kuchen* (coffee and cakes). Rudi did not think there was anything strange in this: Minna impressed on her son that if you had visitors it was only right that you should give them something to eat and drink. It was a straightforward matter of social manners. The half-starved inmates told Minna repeatedly that they liked coming to her house.

Yosef Schwartz was one of the Jewish carpenters who visited SS houses. He may have gone to Dienstweg. "Our job, sometimes, was to fix things in houses… under the supervision of an SS guard – a broken door, a broken shelf, etc. Sometimes we would get some food while 'out on the job'."

One of the inmates who came to the family home made a particularly strong impression on Minna. He was a so-called "house tailor", a man whom Karl had obtained to help his wife with sewing and clothing repairs. It was no inconsiderable task. A Berliner's clothing allowance was meagre. One hundred points was meant to last an adult for eighteen months and a suit took up 80 points – even supposing there was one to be bought. People made and mended, and repaired endlessly.

Over a number of days, the tailor proved to be a quick, adept and polite young man and Minna was minded to help him further. She spoke to her husband and asked if something could be done for him. Could they lighten or shorten his sentence? Karl promised to see what he could do. When he came home that same evening, he said only to Minna that sadly nothing could be done for the tailor, for in the man's records, it stated that he was a murderer.

The reason Karl gave was almost certainly untrue. Dr Astrid Ley of the Sachsenhausen Memorial and Museum said: "I do not think this is possible. Murderers at that time were sentenced to lifelong imprisonment or were executed. The so called 'criminal inmates' in the concentration camp were people with several convictions, mostly for petty crimes, who were deported to a concentration camp immediately after they had served their sentence. People convicted for capital crimes did not come to the camps. The statement probably was some excuse, either by Niemann to explain to his wife why he failed to help or by the SS man whom Niemann asked for this favour."

On some Sundays, a special visitor would come to eat with the family. If there was meat (a rare thing) available that week, it would be kept to share with the guest. A thin man who spoke with an Austrian accent, he was otherwise like Karl; he worked in the same Berlin office and wore the same *Hauptsturmführer* uniform. But Rudi had been told something that made the man an object of some fascination. It was said that this man had been an inmate of a concentration camp and that Rudi's father had had him released to work for him. More than likely, the children were instructed beforehand not to ask questions.

Round about the time when war broke out, a special gang of slave labourers was brought in. Most Berliners turned their cellars into makeshift bomb shelters – reinforcing them with wooden joists. Karl went one step further – he had inmates build bunk beds and fit them against the walls of the cellar. In the unlikely event of a night-time air raid, the family would have a tolerable degree of comfort in their underground cell. And in that first year of victories, it did seem unlikely that they would ever be needed. Göring boasted that if a single enemy bomber reached Germany, they could call him Meier.*

Though fighting was far away in those early days, the war did have a significant impact right from the start. On the very first day of hostilities, it plunged the Zehlendorf settlement – quite literally – into darkness. Blackout restrictions were imposed on 1st September 1939 throughout the capital. Every night thereafter, the family had to close the outside shutters and roll down blackout blinds over the windows. Rudi remembered carrying torches with tiny slits and filters over the beams, and seeing cars in the streets whose filtered headlights barely glowed through small rectangular slots. And there were very few cars – Germany had one of the lowest rates of car ownership in Europe. Though they lived in a city, after dusk they might as well have been in a tiny village, the terraced house among pines a place of total darkness and near silence.

Even before the war had begun, a spectre from the Great War reappeared on the scene. Rationing was introduced in the last week of August 1939. Food, clothing, even coal became subjected to restrictions and the family's ration cards became as valuable as money itself.

Supplies of coffee, that essential luxury for most Germans, soon ground to a halt, to be replaced by ersatz products. One was pulverised chicory, the other malt, which went by the appealing name of *Muckefuck*. Rudi developed a liking for *schmalz*, rendered goose fat which was served instead of butter. *Schmalz* had been a traditional ingredient in German homes, and still was in Jewish cookery.

Ever the thrifty improviser, Minna made *Falscher Pfannkuchen*

---

* A very common German name. The British equivalent of the saying might be "if this happens, you can call me Mr Smith". Witty Berliners called air raid sirens that *did* herald the arrival of bombers "Meier's trumpets".

(mock pancakes), an approximation of the celebrated Berlin filled egg pastry, only this had no filling and no eggs.

The government had a dictatorship's habit of announcing that bad things were good. It decreed that, once a month, every family should "enjoy" an *Eintopf* – an all-in-one stew, which consisted of every available scrap being thrown in the pot and cooked for an inordinate length of time until softened. "*Eintopf*?" said Rudi, wrinkling his face in disgust. "Yes, I remember that."

For those at the top of the Nazi hierarchy, rationing made no difference. Both Göring and Goebbels dined at a top restaurant in Berlin, where nothing was ever off the menu. A number of ministers had a hand in a thriving black market. Minna urged Karl to use his own connections in the SS to obtain forbidden luxuries for the family. "Get us some chicken," she would say. Karl flatly refused: "If *they* don't have chicken," he said, gesturing flamboyantly towards the window, "then *we* don't have chicken either."

Karl's principled stand wobbled just a little when it came to his children. Every now and then, chocolate would appear. Minna would hand a little piece to each child with the wise admonition: "Eat it here in the house, not in the street. If other children see it and get no chocolate, it will break their hearts." The invasion of Russia brought war booty back and into the Zehlendorf living room. Heavy smoker Anne was supplied with wickedly strong Russian cigarettes in cardboard tubes that she would squeeze between her fingers to provide the barest of filters.

One of the tiresome consequences of rationing was that long periods of queuing for pretty much everything became standard procedure. Mutti became accustomed to hurrying off at any time when news came through of some item that was about to be available for sale. On an irregular basis, the youngsters were used to being home alone.

In the early years of the war, air raid sirens sent the family down to the cellar. Göring's assurances about Luftwaffe invincibility were tested almost a year into the fighting. The first Allied bombing attack took place in August 1940 and raids continued sporadically into the autumn. Though Zehlendorf escaped unscathed and the damage to the rest of city was relatively light, the duration of the raids had a psychological effect. Late at night, Berliners would be sent down to their cellars for four hours at a time. Wrapped up in their bunks and with their children's capacity to sleep through anything, it may not have been that big a deal for the little Niemann boys once the novelty had worn off. Rudi and Eki remembered nothing of sheltering in their cellar: their memories of bomb shelters come from much later when they were in a place where the war had a much greater impact.

For Karl and Minna's two youngest sons, war was the only way of life they knew. Rudi was five and a half when Germany invaded Poland; Eki was eighteen months old. Nearly six years of their young lives would be swallowed up in a constrained, peculiarly adapted existence that was, to them, the norm. Yet these were boys with irrepressibly mischievous personalities and the oddities and restrictions imposed by adults only seemed to push them into deeper transgressions. They rebelled by being children – and very naughty ones at that.

Rudi was six years old when he was sent off carrying a little leather satchel to the *U-Bahn* station at Krumme Lanke. Every day, he took the underground to the neighbouring suburb of Dahlem. If he learned anything at school there, it was the art of cunning. One teacher, standing with his back to the class while he wrote on the blackboard, would swivel at the sound of a voice and hurl chalk in the direction of the offender. Another would walk among the desks and swipe at a miscreant with whatever he had to hand.

In both cases, Rudi learned when to duck, so that the boy behind him got it.

When school was over, Rudi played outside with any children he could find. They had precious few toys, but there was no limit to a child's imagination: "We made guns out of sticks. And we'd pick something up and say, 'now this is not a piece of wood, it's a hand grenade'. And it *was* a hand grenade. We played war games all the time. And we always won."

On rainy days and in the evenings, Rudi would pore over the postcard-sized magazines he had collected, a series that included editions on fighting in Africa. And postcard-sized photographs of his heroes. Germany had gone into celebrity overdrive. Its stars were the victors of recent military campaigns. They were feted publicly and publicity materials poured out to satisfy the appetites of young enthusiasts. Rudi listed Ernst Udet, a flying ace from the Great War, Günther Prien, a U-boat captain who shot to fame at the beginning of the war when he led a daring raid into a British harbour, and tank ace Erwin Rommel as his favourites.

Eki, a dark-haired child in a family of Aryan blondes, was a sunny-natured boy with a reputation for fearsome tear tantrums. Minna's sailor brother Heinrich, a regular visitor to the family home, once plotted to capture one of Eki's toddler storms on camera by giving him a cutlet bone (a particular favourite for a child in love with gnawing), and then taking it away again. The ruse worked perfectly.

Eki began an accident-prone career of misadventures as a toddler. One of his earliest memories was of being parked in his high chair on the terrace outside the back door: "This high chair had a pisspot integrated under the seat. A sneaky little neighbour, a little older than I, crept up and tried to lovingly bite my bare toes. I didn't much like that, so I began to rock the chair. The chair toppled over and I cut my forehead when I hit the ground. Besides the pain, I had also tipped the contents of the bowl all down my neck. A few years later, I wanted to take revenge for this despicable act. I lured the said young lady into our bunker. When I tried to kiss her, I was caught out and given such a spanking."

One day, when Eki could still barely walk, he saw his father coming up the path and tried to clamber up the patio door to greet him, but only managed to put his foot through the glass. In the dining room of their house, there stood a big oven with a long stovepipe: "In winter, it would always be properly heated and then the stovepipe would be red hot. 'You must not touch it or you will burn yourself' – I still have that in my ears. But of course, and perhaps just because it was forbidden, I had to try it out and my scream could be heard through the whole house."

Karl's eldest son Dieter was a comic-book Aryan, a Charlie Brown lookalike with big ears that stuck out, a babyish kiss curl and a permanently downturned mouth that appeared desperate to break into a snigger. He was a sharp-shooting member of the Hitler Youth, earning the HJ proficiency award for his military, sports and political prowess. A target pinned up next to the kitchen window testified to his practice with an air rifle. That the glass stayed intact suggests he was a competent shot.

Though he had an education soaked in Nazi indoctrination, Dieter shared some of his siblings' playful, cock-a-snook-at-authority characteristics. When people bandied around references to the German people as the *Herrenvolk* (the master race), he responded with a name he had invented, a compound noun which translates as "the so-called shit of the earth". He gave nicknames to his mother, brothers and sister. Minna was Tuschen (the name has no meaning), Anne was Nuschen (still no meaning), Rudi was rechristened Rolli and Eki went by the moniker Nudel (noodle). There was no term of endearment for his father, with whom he had a difficult, argumentative relationship. Minna said ruefully that the pair "fought like brothers".

Dieter was forthright and unconventional, a vegetarian in pig-loving Germany. Eki was told that his big brother doted on him as a baby and toddler. Mother and son had an especially close bond. Minna always called Dieter her "big boy". She made a suit for Dieter's confirmation when he was fifteen. When it came to religion, Minna's view prevailed over Karl's. Her big boy was confirmed in the Lutheran Church.

Most of all, Dieter had a passion for the arts. Rudi remembered him as "very clever, always looking for books and things to read". Dieter would always be sitting reading, twirling his hair with his fingers over and over. Once Rudi and Eki took the bold step of going into a bookshop when they were still small and bought him a book they thought he would like. Generous-hearted Dieter did an almost perfect job of convincing them that he was delighted with their purchase.

The younger brothers did not see much of their older sister. Anne studied at school with the ambition of becoming a cookery teacher. In 1941, on her eighteenth birthday, German forces on the Eastern Front were within a few miles of taking Moscow. Anne, meanwhile, was heading west. She had begun her *Landfrauenjahr*, the compulsory year of service in which girls left the cities to work on the land. It was a particular passion of Hitler, who believed a year in the country would give young urban women proper affinity with *Blut und Erde* (blood and soil). Anne served her time on a farm in a hamlet called Gross Berkel near Hameln, working for a farmer friend of the Niemann family.

While in the Hameln district, Anne attended the wedding of cousin Ursel, a high-cheeked, long-necked beauty about three years older than herself. Fräulein Borcherding was marrying into the SS élite, her husband-to-be a member of the Hitler SS Leibstandarte, a regiment that was nominally Hitler's own personal bodyguard.

At the church, the racial pedigree of both sides of the union was laid out before the congregation. The groom's family tree stretched in an unblemished line back to 1750. "Why does ours end here?" asked Anne archly, pointing to a trail of Schwenker ancestors that stopped short. The answer was uttered just loud enough for Anne alone to hear – sometime back in the early 1800s, an ancestor had been a Jewish horse trader. But the family secret was kept hidden well enough on the day and Ursel became a new bride. Not long after, her husband was posted back to the Russian front, and not long after that, the unfortunate Ursel – by now pregnant – found herself a widow.

It seems that while she was working on the land, Anne herself fell in love. At eighteen years of age, she became attached to a flight sergeant in the Luftwaffe. The pilot her brothers remembered only as Hans-Rudi came to the house in Berlin to see her parents. The couple became engaged, but very shortly after, Anne suffered the same fate as her cousin. Hans-Rudi was killed in battle. Anne kept a picture of him ever after. A wavy-haired, light-eyed young man with a pleasing upturned mouth, one hand thrust casually in his pocket, looks back at the photographer – probably Anne herself – with an air of mild amusement.

Dieter now filled a hole in his sister's life. He and Anne went into the city to the theatre; they were avid cinemagoers too. They grew ever closer, linked arms. Theirs was an affectionate, normal relationship in very abnormal circumstances.

Minna was the pivotal figure in the family. She had a talent for organisation and a common-sense wisdom that made her a confessional figure for her brood. Eki described her as a true friend. It seemed as if she was the boss in the house. Karl never contradicted Minna in front of the children. But Rudi observed that she ruled "only as far as Vati wanted her to".

And Karl? "I never had a Vati," said Rudi. "He was out, always, all over the place. Most of the time, he was away. And then when he got back, he had to get ready for the next trip. I never knew much about him. It's not that I wasn't interested but somehow I think, Vati, he didn't really want to get in touch with anybody else. He wanted to be his own man. And didn't want to get anybody else involved in his business, that's what I think it was, he never talked about anything. It was always Mutti and us."

The child picked up on strains in his parents' relationship during those war years; Karl was a largely absent husband with little connection with his wife. Both Rudi and Eki said their mother hated the Nazis. In the early years, Minna would say: "Himmler is a gangster." "No, no," her husband would counter gently. "He is a good man who only wants the best for Germany." Rudi thought his father was naïve, always wanting to believe the best in everyone. Even gangsters.

Financially, these were good years for Karl. He was earning 13,000 Reichmarks a year, more than double what he had been paid at Dachau. There wasn't much to spend money on during those war years, so, without them knowing, he set up bank accounts for each of his children. It was the act of a prudent money manager.

Karl was a father whose rare interactions with his children during this period were on his terms. The dad who had held the toddler Rudi on his knees and taught him the simple rhyme of the falling rider "*Hoppe Hoppe Reiter*", now picked up Eki and sang a different tune. It was always the same song:

Wenn die Soldaten
Durch die Stadt marschieren,
Öffnen die Mädchen
Die Fenster und die Türen.
Ei warum? Ei darum!
Ei warum? Ei darum!
Ei bloß weg' dem
Schingderassa,
Bumderassasa!
Ei bloß weg' dem
Schingderassa,
Bumderassasa! *

When the soldiers march through the streets
The girls open the windows and the doors
Why is that, just why is that?
Because of the
"Schingderassa
Boomderassa-sa!"
Because of the
"Schingderassa
Boomderassa-sa!"

"*Wenn die Soldaten*" was a jaunty marching song that Karl would have known from his Great War soldiering days. But now it had been re-popularised by the regime and somehow the tune that blared out of the radio as the Wehrmacht marched across Europe, killing and plundering on its way, had lost its innocence.

---

* The sounds are onomatopoeic, representing the drums and cymbals of an army band.

10

In a Nuremberg prison cell, an American doctor sat with a man who would one day be condemned to hang. While the trials of Nazi leaders were taking place in the first half of 1946, Dr Leon Goldensohn was given responsibility for their physical condition. And since he was a trained psychiatrist, he was also tasked with managing their mental health. In between the formal proceedings in the court above, Goldensohn entered into long discussions with the men, who were less guarded out of public scrutiny and with someone who was not part of the official judiciary. Polite, sympathetic and gently probing, the good doctor recorded the interviews he conducted with both defendants and witnesses.

One of those witnesses was Oswald Pohl. The former master of the WVHA issued a predictable litany of lies and evasions. He had had good Jewish friends before the war... though he could not remember their names. Nor could he be held responsible for the atrocities – he offered a curious inverted explanation that they were the actions of the staff beneath him. And like any good boss, he took personal credit for the good work of his subordinates. In this case, he talked about positive action to help concentration camp inmates:

I was inwardly convinced that these internees had to be treated decently. I had internees – not too many, but several – whom I took from the concentration camps because they were good men and good workers. Later on these men became my employees. I was the only one who ever did anything like that. The manager of a plant for making wooden parts for aeroplanes was a former concentration camp internee whom I liberated, and whom I later paid a salary of a thousand marks a month. I didn't have to give him a thousand marks – I could have paid him a hundred marks. Also in Dachau there were other former internees to whom I gave such positions. I did it of my own free will. All of these facts I can prove. I can prove how I thought on the question of internees. Personally, I was humane. Whether the camps themselves were humane is another story, but not my fault.

Whether the doctor believed Pohl is not known. For once, the former manager of SS industries was very nearly telling the truth.

Through most of the war, Karl was a man on the move. His immediate bosses – Gerhard Maurer, Kurt May and, latterly, Josef Opperbeck, largely controlled the woodworking industrial concern from their office desks in Berlin. The two Karls – Niemann and Bestle – were forever on the shop floor. They were both *Geschäftsführer*, business managers whose primary role was to tour the industrial "plants", inspect the quality of production and address difficulties. These "plants" were the concentration camps – including Buchenwald, Dachau, Neuengamme, Ravensbrück, Sachsenhausen and Stutthof – and also a great galaxy of sub-camps. Dachau alone had 123 long-term and temporary sub-camps, including a base at Spitzingsee in the Bavarian Alps, where inmates built wooden log cabins as summer holiday chalets for senior SS officers. Karl would have visited every single camp that had any connection with woodwork production.

The description that Auschwitz *Kommandant* Rudolf Höss gave of their old boss could equally well be applied to the two Karls:

> *Maurer displayed enormous energy in pursuing his main task of obtaining labour for the armaments industry. He travelled a great deal, inspecting the start of an undertaking in one place, or the progress of one somewhere else, or solving difficulties which arose between the individual chiefs and the labour company officers and hearing complaints about the prisoners' work or from the industrial employers about their ill-treatment.*

Dachau concentration camp provides a frightening insight into the lives of the men who worked for the two Karls. On arrival, the business manager from Berlin would meet up with the camp's SS employment officer who "was thoroughly instructed in his task of procuring prison labour for the war industries. This officer also had to make a record of every prisoner's trade or profession and to take strict care that each prisoner was employed according to his abilities."

Karl and Karl had inmates working for them who wanted to be there – that is to say, employed on the least worst jobs within a concentration camp. Any job that involved having a roof over their heads was much sought after. Those inmates who toiled in heavy manual labour outside, such as in quarries, exposed year-round to the elements, at risk of mortal injury, did not live long. The gruelling outdoor work was supervised by a particularly sadistic breed of fellow inmates. Certain inmates were hand-picked by the guards as overseers. Known as *Kapos*, they were given extra rations and – in these situations – ensured their charges were treated brutally. Inmates who answered visiting WVHA officers' questions about their treatment were beaten by the *Kapos* once the men from Berlin had gone. The camp guards approved wholeheartedly of such behaviour.

Bestle and Niemann operated in less vicious surroundings. Yes, they inspected the factory floor – the covered buildings where inmates worked with saws and lathes. But they felt most at home in the concentration camp offices, where administrators like themselves, middle-aged men with wives and children back home, just like them, laboured at desks with pens and balance sheets. These were rated the most desirable jobs in the camp and the employment officer ensured that the "best" inmates worked there. In these offices, out of the sight and hearing of camp guards, the two Karls spoke freely to prisoners.

One of the key figures, a man who would play a significant role in the fate of both Karls, was one of the office-appointed *Kapos*, an Austrian called Franz Müller-Strobl. Back in 1934, Müller-Strobl had resisted an attempt by the Austrian Nazi Party to take power, by fighting against them as a battalion commander. The day after the Anschluss, the annexation of Austria by Hitler in 1938, Nazis with long memories caught up with Müller-Strobl and he was taken into custody. A spell in Flossenbürg concentration camp followed, and assignment to a *Strafkompanie*, a punishment detail where inmates were given even more work, shorter breaks and less food. By the time Müller-Strobl reached Dachau, he was physically broken. But then he had a stroke of luck: "Following Herr Barthel Steiner's* advice, Herr Bestle put me in the office – with that I didn't have to go back into the camp – with my constitution that would have certainly meant death."

Müller-Strobl later told how Bestle helped him further, smuggling out letters and taking them to be delivered in the post office outside. A simple task that, had it been found out, could have been dangerous for the SS man. Another flagrant contravention of the

---

* The SS employment officer at the camp.

rules would certainly have meant much greater trouble for Bestle if he had been caught. In his office routine, Müller-Strobl had been instructed to process *Strafmeldung*, extreme punishment orders for trivial misdemeanours. A few dozen lashes, or a day standing to attention in the open in winter, could mean death for a weakened inmate. Over a period of time, Bestle ordered Müller-Strobl to throw hundreds of these orders away. And both Karls ensured that the men in the offices and those in the workshops received life-saving extra rations – an additional 100g of *wurst* (sausage) and 150g of bread each daily.

More Austrians were brought in to man the office desks. One of them was 42-year-old Franz Doppler from Vienna. A professional engineer, Doppler had worked in Istanbul at a German institute, where he grumbled about restrictions on whom he could employ. Ideologically, Doppler was not necessarily opposed to the Nazis – he had college friends who joined the party and his daughter never knew if her father had been a supporter himself. However, Doppler made a decision to recruit whomever he wanted, irrespective of racial origin. Nazis in Istanbul heard what he was saying, notified the Gestapo in Vienna, and, over a three-year period, the secret police intercepted twenty letters that Doppler sent to his father.

When Doppler went on holiday to visit his parents in Vienna, he was arrested and spent nine months in a Gestapo prison being interrogated. He had, they said, broken the Treachery Act, he had "made negative comments about the Third Reich in letters", he had "mixed with Jews and other immigrant circles" and he was "a reactionary who was very careful" to hide his actions. The shock of hearing that their son had been sent to Dachau killed both of his parents within six months.

Whether it was out of sympathy, an act of pure professional opportunism, or a bit of both, Karl Niemann began to set in motion a remarkable and apparently exceptional train of events. It was known, and accepted, that political prisoners such as Müller-Strobl and Doppler were deemed "capable of improvement". Historically, prisoners had entered "protective custody" for limited periods and were then released when it was decreed they had served their time, and, more importantly, were no longer considered to be a threat to society. The risk of "threat" was too great for this to happen in wartime, so automatic releases did not occur. However, Karl was able to work the system to show that it would be better for these men to work where they could be of more benefit to the state. Quite simply, he had them released to work for him.

Karl entered a bureaucratic minefield that he was adept at negotiating. Though Müller-Strobl and others like him were imprisoned in Dachau, control of their destinies remained in the hands of the Gestapo office which had arrested them in the first place. Karl submitted a request to the Austrian branch of the Gestapo in Klagenfurt and his request was countersigned by Oswald Pohl. As a result, in February 1942, Müller-Strobl found himself on a train to Berlin and started work as Karl's assistant, where he remained to see out the rest of the war.

Here, the story takes an even more bizarre twist. Not only did Müller-Strobl begin working for Karl, he even joined the SS, a poacher turned uniformed gamekeeper at a time when membership of the organisation was not obligatory for workers within the WVHA. He rose to the rank of *Hauptsturmführer* – the same rank as his boss. It was Müller-Strobl who came for Sunday lunch at the Niemanns'; it was for Müller-Strobl that the family saved their weekly meat ration.

Even so, Karl's assistant was never safe from the threat of retribution from those who had previously dragged him into custody. The Gestapo was the malignant puppet master, pulling strings from afar:

"As a political prisoner, I always found myself with different views [from other people]," testified Müller-Strobl. "This also happened in the main office of the DAW in Berlin. Herr Niemann, however, interfered helpfully every time, and protected me from evil… Herr Karl Niemann prevented me from being sent back to a camp in 1943. National Socialist circles from Carinthia [in Austria] were always interested in me, and made the strongest allegations."

Understandably, Müller-Strobl's defection to work for the SS was derided by some fellow inmates. After the war, a Polish inmate called Herbert Slawinski kept up a correspondence with Franz Doppler and was keen to share news about other companions of captivity:

> *I was very interested in your messages about our old fellow sufferers, especially about Müller-Strobl. I always feared, given how fantastic his aversion to everything that leaned to the left was, that he would fall into the arms of the SS… Assertions about Müller-Strobl issuing regulations for the exploitation of inmates in his capacity as an officer of the DAW have not proved groundless.*

Doppler, however, did not shun the benign *Kapo* and old comrade who went to the dark side. He would write to Slawinski using the formal German term of address "*Sie*". Müller-Strobl he addressed with the familiar "*du*". He called him "my dear friend" and urged the Klagenfurt administrator to visit his home. The two men kept in touch until the year Doppler died.

Engineer Doppler had a very good reason for being sympathetic to Müller-Strobl. From his new Berlin office, Müller-Strobl urged Karl to seek the release of Doppler – it appears he also lobbied the highly influential Gerhard Maurer, now based in office D, the office which administered the camps. Maurer – who had got to know

Doppler from camp inspections – approved Karl's request and Karl followed up with the Viennese Gestapo.

Doppler never knew exactly how he had been released, though he always gave credit for the impetus behind it to Müller-Strobl. Eventually, Doppler was employed in a position requiring electronic expertise at the Siemens factory, north of Berlin, and was paid extremely well. But, like Müller-Strobl, he never lost his fear. The Berlin Gestapo began investigating him. The frightened man looked for support from Maurer and the senior SS officer intervened on his behalf. "For the rest of the war, I was left in peace," he commented.

Müller-Strobl affirmed that "Herr Niemann wrote uncountable release requests for political prisoners." There were certainly others at Dachau. Not all were successful. Karl tried to free a fellow Austrian and friend of Doppler, a Salzburg businessman called Karl Steiner. The request was turned down. Steiner said ruefully afterwards that his "crimes" against the Reich were judged too serious. At Buchenwald, a man called Siebold from near Weimar, was released in August 1943 to work for Karl, although no more is known about him.

And then there was Friedrich Naupold…

As a prisoner in Sachsenhausen, I was often sent to office W IV in Berlin-Wannsee to work. During my work there, I got to know Karl Niemann, who had accountancy functions there. We prisoners generally called him "Papa Niemann". I believe that this nickname had a reason, because Papa Niemann was to all, whether prisoner, or civil employee, the same benevolent man. Rarely have I met a man like Papa Niemann among the SS members. In short: open, Christian character, always ready to help and show understanding for everyone and every situation.

Herr Niemann – with whom I often spoke over the years – note as a prisoner! – that was not only for me but also for Niemann forbidden and dangerous* – tried eventually, upon my speaking with him, to free me from the camp.

That these attempts [to free me] not only caused Herr N. much trouble and inconvenience as a SS member, I need not emphasise here.

In any case, Herr Niemann managed, after fighting for a year, to get me released from Sachsenhausen and given work. Because without work, my release wouldn't have happened!

I am thus extraordinarily grateful to Herr Niemann, because, put simply…he saved my life, because I wouldn't have lived another six months with my physical constitution in the camp!!

There was one task beyond him. Karl may have known that it was beyond his power to free the polite and helpful tailor who came to the Niemann household to assist his wife. The get-out-of-jail card was only available to political prisoners. The other unfortunates who had the wrong racial background, orientation or beliefs – the Jews, homosexuals and Jehovah's Witnesses, had no prospect at all of release.

For one of the concentration camps, there are no records at all. Karl swore in a court of law that he never went there, and there was nothing in writing to contradict him. Before its liberation by Russian soldiers, every piece of paper connected with the camp was burned. Only the oral testimonies from survivors are left, and

---

* Sachsenhausen archivist Dr Astrid Ley points out that the "danger" was wildly exaggerated. As a *Hauptsturmführer*, Karl would have outranked just about every SS officer in a concentration camp. He could pretty much do and say what he liked.

nobody mentioned the name of Karl Niemann when they told of their experiences in the death camp that was Auschwitz.

Witnesses certainly remembered Oswald Pohl. He was the living bogeyman. They told how gold, including fillings extracted from the teeth of murdered inmates, was put in railway trucks. The booty that was transported back to Berlin was known euphemistically among the inmates as "presents for Pohl". One man recalled seeing Pohl standing for some time at a spyhole to watch Jews being gassed. Pohl admitted – there was photographic evidence – to visiting Auschwitz twice. But what about Karl?

Holocaust specialist Dr Jan Erik Schulte believes it is inconceivable that Karl did not go there. Karl would admit in court to travelling to both Lublin and Lemberg a couple of times – camps that were still farther to the east. Auschwitz was the DAW's second-biggest factory behind Dachau – in October 1942 alone, its inmates built 3,000 triple-tier bunk beds. In the following year, it turned in a profit of more than half a million Reichmarks. It stretches credulity to think that a man who so assiduously went again and again to the sites for which he bore responsibility, went to smaller, less accessible locations, but did not drop in at a key location only a few hours by train from Berlin.

Even if we accept Karl at his word, he was, nevertheless, a regular at many of the other centres of depravity. Historian Schulte said vehemently: "He would have had to be blind not to have seen evidence of mass killing." There were gas chambers, smoking crematoria, lines of inmates by the railway tracks, skeletal figures by the barrack huts, men hanging from makeshift gallows, or tied by their wrists, piles of discarded clothing, the stench of decaying and burning bodies.

Karl's colleague Bestle went so far as to say publicly during the war that he had seen and heard nothing. A post-war investigator quizzed Bestle's Berlin neighbours:

In personal conversations with tenants of the houses, who told him about the cruelties and crimes in the concentration camps, it could be seen that he never believed in those crimes and always considered them as lies. He told them in response that he wasn't only working at Sachsenhausen and Buchenwald, but also at other camps as construction manager and never saw anything of the sort.

11

Shortly after his seventeenth birthday, Dieter was taken out of school to defend his country on the home front. Like all the other boys in his class, he was given automatic passes in all subjects. It was a fate that befell tens of thousands of teenagers, who paid the price for an inevitable downturn in the Reich's fortunes. In February 1943, nearly 200,000 soldiers of the Wehrmacht surrendered at Stalingrad. It was the first decisive defeat of the war. In North Africa, the Afrika Korps was in retreat. Rommel wrote to his wife: "There's going to be total mobilisation for every German, without regard for place of residence, status, property or age." The letter proved prescient: on 18th February, Goebbels gave a speech in Berlin's Sportpalast promising Germany total war.*

Along with all his schoolmates, Dieter had been conscripted three days earlier to serve as an anti-aircraft auxiliary, a *Flakhelfer*. Men of fighting age were shipped off to the front and boy soldiers took their place. The government called them cadets, hoping that

---

* A complete subordination of all activity, both military and civilian, to war ends. Goebbels meant it also in the sense of giving no quarter and imposing no restraints.

the name could disguise from the Allies the fact that Germany was now relying on children to fill the army's depleted ranks. Though he still wore the badge and armband of a youth organisation, Dieter donned the steel helmet of a soldier when the enemy aircraft came.

Round about the time when Dieter was called up, Karl decided the family cellar was not a safe place in which to hide from the bombs. It was not the prospect of structural damage that worried him, but the risk caused by the gas pipes that ran through the bottom of the house. Even the slightest nick might cause a gas leak and the family would be suffocated. Karl drummed up a team of labourers from the concentration camp to build the family an air raid shelter in the common land just beyond the end of the garden. Rudi stood at an upstairs window and watched them dig an enormous hole deep in the sand, then fill it with a huge wooden frame. The men put in steps leading down to the inner sanctuary and the box was covered with a thick dome of sand. When the job was complete, Anne and Grete, the family's maid, tested its strength by sitting on top and posed for their picture.

Berlin's position deep within a conquered continent meant that German intelligence could give its citizens due warning that the bombers were coming. The bulk of the populace relied on *Draht-funk*, a radio transmission that went down the telephone wires once conventional radio had been closed down. The code words *Gustav Heinrich* told the listener that enemy aircraft were approaching Berlin. Karl's connections gave the family access to a still more sophisticated early warning system called *Flaksender*:

"Vati had a map, which divided Germany up into squares, and the forecast said when the [enemy] forces came in. We knew where they were, we knew which square, and we knew where we were sitting, so we could say, ah, they are about so many kilometres away so we'd better go down to the bunker now," explained Rudi.

Minna concentrated the minds of her children for the nightly expeditions to the bottom of the garden: "When the alarm siren wailed – and who could forget such a dreadful wail in their life? – we had to go quickly into the bunker. Every one of us had the task of taking something valuable with us from the house into the bunker. We never knew whether we would see our house again after the raid, whether everything would be undamaged and inhabitable. Little me always had to lug the small case containing the silver service," said Eki.

Before long, Karl had extended the hospitality of the bunker to the family's neighbours – a mother and her two grown-up daughters. Bags of Niemann valuables were left in the house to make way for the extra occupants. "The bunker was so cramped that people were stuck together, knee to knee," recalled Eki. "When the bombs fell, we heard Wheeee! Vvvvvom! Wheee! Vvvvvooom!" As white-haired Eki made the sound of each explosion, his shoulders juddered, shaking as perhaps only someone who had actually lived through such an experience would do with the memory.

There was the very real risk that the family would be blown to bits or buried alive. The instinct for self-preservation made them clutch at one piece of received wisdom circulating around the Berlin estates: "When the bombs fell – you could tell that from the loud wails from above outside – then came the command at once – '*Macht den Mund auf!*' (open your mouth wide!) The reason given for that was to balance the impact of the explosion in your head; otherwise it could burst your eardrums," said Eki. Once, bombs shrieked and exploded close by. Five-year-old Eki looked into the face of the petrified neighbour sitting opposite and said in all innocence: "Frau Finger, you look very funny with your mouth open so wide."

On nights when he was off work, Dieter joined his family in the bunker. Much to his mother's consternation, he was always last down the steps. Casually fearless, he was used to seeing the firework show out in the open on those nights when he manned the big guns. Dieter could not resist staying above ground to watch coloured flares from the bombers lighting up the sky, the shooting spears of searchlight beams, and, all the while, hearing the boom-boom from the ack-ack – the guns of his own post.

One night, Dieter mistimed his watch. A bomb exploded with an ear-deafening crash only feet away and he was blown down the steps of the bunker. Both he and his family down below survived because the shell had lodged in a pine tree that overshadowed the shelter. In the morning, the family inspected the tree, its crown blown off, leaving only a trunk with a shredded top.

Rudi followed his brother's bad example by sometimes slipping out in the middle of a raid himself to see what was happening outside – "We all did," he said. Though he could not see the pathfinder planes in the darkness, he could see their work, as they dropped lights out of the sky – "Christmas trees, we called them." The flares illuminated the ground below, giving the bombers a target to aim at.

The British planes came at night. And thankfully for the Berliners, their raids were mercifully short. There was no need for bunk beds (not that there was any room in the garden bunker) or naps on the benches wedged up against their neighbours. The alerts rarely lasted more than an hour. But by early 1944, there was a new routine as American bombers arrived by day. "It was always at the same time; you could set your clock by it," said Rudi. He stood at the top of the bunker steps and watched. "I saw them out there, all of them, because especially at the beginning they were always flying in formation, and they had hundreds of aircraft. And we were standing out there once and there was an American, pretty high up. It was there and then pft! Gone. Exploded. Hit. All gone. One of these big Flying Fortress things. Just exploded."

American bombers lingered in the skies far longer than the RAF; it might be two or three hours before a raid was over. Whenever the children came out of the bunker after the estate had suffered bomb damage, it was to the exciting prospect of a new landscape, a pock-marked playground. One bomb had left a massive crater between the back gardens of Dienstweg 19 and the house next door. Here was a sandbox of stupendous proportions. Rudi and Eki rushed down to play in the crater. "What beautiful serpentine roads we were able to make to drive our toy cars on," sighed Eki.

Another giant crater provided "entertainment" for the whole estate. Rudi hit on the idea of gathering up all the dead wood they could find. He and his friends collected every branch, bush, small tree and anything else that looked combustible and began to fill the crater. When the crater was full to overflowing, one bright spark got to work with matches. Soon there was a huge bonfire. Night was falling and the British were expected. Here was a blazing beacon, a target for the bombers. Adults from all the houses around became alerted to the result of the children's game. They rushed out of their doors and began to throw sand on the fire to put it out. "Oh, I got it when I got home, though. I wasn't hit or anything but I was told not to do that again!"

As the elder of the two scamps, Rudi was sometimes given a job as Dieter's little helper. When he had time off from his duties as ack-ack auxiliary, Dieter would scour the estate looking for unexploded incendiary bombs and then dump them in a crater and render them safe. "He knew there was a colour coding on the bombs – which ones were explosives and which ones were incendiaries. He got us to collect all the incendiaries that hadn't gone off. He would pick one out, bang it on the ground and it would explode. And then he would pile all the other ones on top and it was a lovely bonfire," said Rudi. One incendiary had gone off but never made it to the ground. Rudi remembered it wedged in the crown of a pine tree, smouldering away for hours.

Some craters needed to be left well alone. "The Yanks had been, and they had dropped a land mine. We knew where it was because there was a big crater – you could see where it had gone down. We all had to go home because of the delayed fuse – we didn't know when it would go off. And then it did go off. But Berlin was *die Streubüchse des Pruessisches Landes* [the sandbox of the country], because it was sand, just sand, nothing else. This bleedin' thing went down, and down, and down and then exploded and I think just lifted a few tiles, nothing else. But the crater, it was colossal!"

The boys found delight in treasure that rained down from the skies. They looked for the tail fins of bombs and Rudi took up a new hobby as a shrapnel collector. Showers of twisted shards of metal came from shells fired out by the city's own ack-ack guns. Rudi gathered up pieces and took them upstairs, spreading them out on his bedroom floor. What did his mother think of that? "She didn't seem to mind."

Rudi and Eki never went into the city centre during the war years. But they had some awareness that the heart of the capital was being destroyed: "After one of the big attacks, when you looked down into the city you couldn't see anything. Everything was black, because the clouds of smoke were being blown over to our area. There was so much smoke that it covered the sun, everything," mused Rudi. Otherwise, they knew things were bad when extra rations of coffee were announced, for the authorities always dished out a few grams more after heavy raids.

There came a time when the SS estate itself was carpet-bombed. A short while before, Karl had repaired a broken window pane on his cold frame. He placed a flat-bottomed boulder on top to hold it in place. He had also sent Dieter up on the roof to take down one of the two layers of beaver-tail tile cladding and store the tiles in the cellar.

About 60 bombs pounded down on the estate. The family emerged from the bunker afterwards to find every window on the estate smashed, every roof with all of its tiles dislodged. And Vati's cold-frame boulder had been blown out of the garden and was now sitting on the very top of the roof.

Nine-year-old Rudi led a team of young air raid wardens on a mission. Water from burst mains was pouring down the streets, so they gathered tiles and bits of rubble and made walkways for people to cross without getting their feet wet. Yet even though so many bombs had fallen, they had landed in the trees, in the gardens and on the common open areas. Only one house was actually hit. The adults filled the broken window frames with cardboard. That same day Dieter descended into the cellar to collect the stored tiles and then scrambled up a ladder. By nightfall, Dienstweg 19 was the only house around with a complete set of tiles on its roof.

During the entire war, more than 20,000 Berliners were killed in air raids, and one-third of the city's houses were rendered uninhabitable. But nobody died on the SS estate, and only one family lost their home. Perhaps this was because the estate had been built on the edge of the Grunewald among pine trees that had largely been left standing and these hid the houses from the bombers above.

Less than a hundred yards from the estate, across the Argentinische Allee in the older part of town, an English doctor named Christabel Bielenberg[*] observed a very different scene: "Although I knew Zehlendorf well, I could not recognise a single landmark. Since I had been there last, every house, every street had changed its

---

[*] Bielenberg was author of *The Past is Myself*, an autobiographical account of life in wartime Germany with her anti-Nazi German lawyer husband, Peter.

face. Boarded windows, heaps of rubble, walls blown in, blown out, blown away, like open-fronted dolls' houses they disclosed sudden intimate glimpses of furnishings and decorations within."

The garden of Dienstweg 19 had been turned into a sandy desert. Karl and Dieter set to work digging, so that they could grow strawberries, just as they had the summer before.

12

Karl sat at his desk, engaged in a massive undertaking. He was no longer in the offices at Unter den Eichen – they had been bombed so badly during a raid in the spring of 1943 that they were unusable. Instead, 35 employees were crammed into a barrack hut, put up hastily on Dreilindenstrasse,* close to a huge lake called the Wannsee.

Karl had not long agreed a new contract of employment, entitling him to 35 days' leave, a generous pension and allowances to his wife and children should he die in service. He was now earning the very comfortable salary of 1,100 Reichsmarks a month. Oswald Pohl signed off Karl's contract with his trademark thick black signature. Karl's career was nicely renewed. It was as if life in the DAW would just go on and on.

The auditor in Karl once more played the role he knew and loved. He marshalled armies of figures, lined them up in columns, adding explanatory detail to the numbers to create a coherent whole. His task, in those winter days of early 1944, was to prepare the annual accounts.

---

* It translates as the street of three lime trees.

Here was a summary of the workings of the SS holding company and its various industries over a twelve-month period. Much of what he wrote would pass for ordinary in any set of company accounts:

Executive officers of the companies

1   *Josef Opperbeck – Director*

2   *Karl Niemann – Manager*
    Karl Bestle – Manager

3   *Walter Reinartz – Confidential clerk for the entire administration*
    Franz Müller-Strobl – Confidential clerk for the entire administration
    Rudolf Wagner – Confidential clerk for the entire administration

We can imagine Karl taking special pride in drawing bar charts, filling in blocks showing years of mounting success, headed with the title "Development of turnover 1941 till 1943". It was the chance for the auditor to demonstrate rapid expansion – 5.4 million Reichmarks in 1941, 9.5 million in 1942 and 23.2 million in 1943. The figures were topped off with "a net profit for the year of 1.6 million RM".

The standard costs that any company would incur on behalf of its staff were listed: "Health insurance, insurance against invalidity, employees' insurance, payment of pensions etc". And extra liabilities given the war situation: "support to family members of employees called up for military service".

The workforce had increased fourfold in just three years:

Average number of persons employed 1941 till 1943

1941
218 Employees
3,650 Inmates
Persons employed: 3,868

1942
276 Employees
7,402 Inmates
Persons employed: 7,678

1943
485 Employees and workers
15,498 Inmates
Persons employed: 15,983

Such a huge workforce came cheaply. Wages for 15,498 prisoners were calculated at 6,106,521 Reichsmarks. Each prisoner was paid 394 Reichmarks a year, just over 7.5 a week. What the figures omitted to say was that the inmates received not a pfennig of these tiny wage packets – all of the money was paid to the government.

Karl outlined the scale of SS enterprises: "In 1943 the company owned the following plants: Auschwitz, Bachmanning, Buchenwald, Dachau, Fürstenwalde, Lemberg, Lublin, Neuengamme, Ravensbrück, Sachsenhausen, Sword-forge Dachau, Stutthof... The production of all these plants is characterised by the fact that they are exclusively engaged in armaments contracts and essential war work ordered by public authorities for the completion of special war tasks."

The plants were defined purely in terms of their profitability: Dachau 709,000 Reichsmarks, Auschwitz 568,000, Sachsenhausen

453,000, Buchenwald 427,000, and so on. There was room and ideas for improvement:

As a commercial-technical innovation it may be mentioned that from the beginning of 1944, audit boards will be instituted in all of the plants – for the purpose of rationalising our costings and checking the profitability of our works on the lines of rules applicable to the system of free enterprise to force the plants to strict economy, as it must be required today more than ever.

Even a statement of accounts cannot hide alarming aberrations, such as "A payment of 6,910 to the Gestapo at Dachau". To do what? More disturbing still was a single item tucked within a random list of products. It was an entry that would be well understood by Karl's superiors without any need for more explanation (the item is highlighted below in bold).

300,000 ammunition boxes, cartridge boxes and field boxes, 130,000 various pieces of furniture manufactured (cupboards, tables, double beds, guard beds and stools), 70,000 windows and doors, 550,000 brush handles, 310,000 wooden soles, 100,000 wooden spoons, 390,000 pairs of wooden shoes with upper part of leather made, 325,000 articles of military clothing (coats, uniforms, labour dresses, underwear), 36,000 rifles and side-arms repaired, 2,950,000 gun cartridges repaired, 5,000 bomb rings for the Luftwaffe repaired, 15,500,000 different printed forms manufactured, **6 railway carriages of clothes cleaned and mended for the Intermediate Station for Racial Germans…**

Six railway carriages represents an awful lot of clothes from an awful lot of people. We might look to find the corresponding six railway carriages of inmates' striped uniforms on the debit side. But we would look in vain. In that year, hundreds of thousands took their clothes off, and never lived to put any on again.

An equally chilling and illuminating picture wrapped in euphemisms appears some way down the accounts:

Completion of planned and approved new constructions were completely written off. Apart from the normal deductions, extraordinary deductions were made in Lublin, on account of the special conditions created by the developing military situation, as well as with consideration of the results of the special action of 3rd November 1943.

The Polish town of Lublin (and its principal concentration camp of Majdanek, where most inmates were interned) was some way from the front at that time. What was the "special action" (the German phrase is *Sonderaktion*) that happened on that particular day? Further on, Karl states:

The turnover figure is greatly influenced by the special action carried through in the Lublin and Lemberg plants at the beginning of November 1943, which brought these plants to a complete standstill. A turnover of about 2 million RM was lost through the closing down of these works and the ensuing loss of about 8,000 workers for the months of November and December.

Eight thousand lost workers? Where did they go? A year and a half later, an unknown American lawyer at Nuremberg involved in the trial of Oswald Pohl and his associates would pick up on this paragraph. He would write: "Interrogation on the extent and meaning of this measure is suggested". And well he might.

The majority of people in Germany had no inkling of what was taking place in occupied Poland that autumn. It was kept as a matter of strict secrecy. Those in the immediate district of the "special action" had a pretty good idea. At dawn on 3rd November, the SS initiated *Aktion Erntefest* (Operation Harvest Festival). The "crop" being harvested over the next two days was 42,000 Jews. They included (and Karl had the number) 8,000 Jews from the concentration camps, who were taken outside the camps, shot and buried in trenches. Music blared from loudspeakers to drown out the sounds of the massacre.

Karl concluded the accounts on an optimistic note:

The fact that in 1943 we were able to cope with all the tasks set out to us is above all to the merit of our working staff and we wish to express our gratitude and appreciation for their unselfish readiness for service.

In order to promote the readiness for service of the camp inmates as well, efficiency bonuses were set up, by which particularly remarkable results were achieved.

All of the plants of the German Equipment Works GmbH* have been mobilised to their full capacity to produce armaments and carry out essential war work. Apart from the production of serial goods in the wood-processing and iron-processing branches of industry, they are doing important repair work and are producing goods as subcontractors.

Thus the German Equipment Works GmbH endeavours to make in their own way their obligatory contribution to victory!

---

* Abbreviation for *Gesellschaft mit beschränkter Haftung*, a company with limited liability.

13

"Is this a pen?" asked Fräulein Teppich.

"Yes," answered nine-year-old Rudi, slowly. "This is a pen."

Those were his first words of English but they were not uttered in the classroom of his school in Dahlem. The desks had given way to beds, the pupils to men without arms and legs. The boys' school had been turned into a hospital for wounded soldiers. Eki had been in his class for just a few days or weeks – long enough for him to learn how to shape his letters, but not long enough for the teachers to shape him into a good little Nazi. Such education as the boys now had took place in the family dining room: "A little private thing my father arranged," said Rudi. "Just a few of us – he knew the teacher."

Rudi remembered another encounter with Fräulein Teppich outside his home in what passed for normal Berlin. By early 1944, Anne had an office job, "something to do with helping the soldiers," thought Rudi. Goebbels had closed down Berlin's theatres the year before, but the propaganda minister, a fanatical cinemagoer, had kept the big screens going. Anne and Dieter went as often as possible, and they often sent their little brother two stops down the line of the Berlin underground to the incongruously named Onkel Toms Hütte (Uncle Tom's Cabin), where he would queue for them. Bored Rudi always took a book to pass the time. "By the way, the black is the lettering and the white is the paper," came a voice. It was Fräulein Teppich. Rudi pretended not to notice.

On Rudi's tenth birthday in March it became compulsory for him to attend the Deutsches Jungvolk, the junior section of the Hitler Youth. "They were great ones for sport, always sport. And marching. I had better things to do than just walking about. There was rifle shooting too, but that was only for the older boys, those in the Hitler Youth." Hitler's own enthusiasm for teaching young boys to stamp on weakness filtered down to these meetings in a Berlin suburb, where there were elements of cruelty and sadism. Rudi carried an abiding memory of being passed and pummelled between two rows of boys.

Salvation for him came from an unexpected direction. Air raids had disrupted and finally curtailed evening Jungvolk meetings, so that they were now held on Sundays. Before long, Karl went to the group leader and told him that his son would no longer be attending: "That is the day when I am at home and I want my son round the table with me," he insisted. Rudi always believed it was a brave and dangerous thing for his father to do. But perhaps a mere youth leader would have had no comeback against a captain of the SS.

Rudi spent much of his time roaming around the neighbour-hood. A cluster of friends included a boy whose father had been invalided out of the army. When the father thought nobody was looking, his limp miraculously disappeared. This wounded soldier was a tobacconist. His son stole cigarillos from the shop and the boys stood on a bridge over the railway line pretending to smoke them, so that train passengers could see just how grown-up they were.

In July 1944 an event occured that had an impact on every Berlin-er's life. A group of army officers tried – and very nearly succeeded – in blowing up Hitler at his East Prussian headquarters. The reper-cussions of Operation Valkyrie, the failed bomb plot led by Claus von Stauffenberg, were felt countrywide – even in Zehlendorf. The Gestapo was looking for suspects. The estate was gripped by fear, bewilderment and suspicion. Posters suddenly appeared in the streets. They carried messages that Rudi did not quite understand and photographs of men he did not recognise. The posters simply said – "Have you seen this man?" It was typical unsettling Nazi propaganda, persuading the majority to turn against the disloyal, implying the guilt of those portrayed without being explicit.

Rudi's mind followed a child's irrefutable logic. He marshalled his little gang and they marched out into the streets. They went round and took down every single poster. After all, if they wanted him to find these men, then he would need to know and remember what they looked like. "We were all running around trying to find these wanted men, you know. But we never found them."

That summer, Rudi had a new companion on his adventures. At six years old, Eki was a pain, but by now a mobile one, and a passable playmate when there was no one else around. The two boys explored dark corners of the house when all the grown-ups were out. They found their father's regimental sword from the First World War languishing at the back of their parents' wardrobe, and paraded it round the room. Rudi sniffed the scabbard, breathing in the stink of old leather. They put the sword back carefully. Would their father have approved of them playing with his weapon? "Oh no. He would not have been amused at all."

Their habitual playground was the Krumme Lanke lake, a five-minute dash from the house through the woods. They ferreted through the undergrowth as children do and made a miraculous discovery: "In the bushes, we found a whole stash of rifles. There were some old muzzle-loaders from the time of Frederick the Great but also some reasonably modern ones. Rudi had found himself a Tesching handgun. I kept an old muzzle-loader. We carried them home as booty," said Eki.

Their parents were not best pleased, and confiscated the weapons at once. The most likely explanation for the woodland arsenal was that someone had got rid of them out of fear for what the enemy would do when it found them in their home. By now, there were plenty of people who no longer believed in the much-trumpeted *Endsieg* (final victory).

Eki raced around the estate on the scooter he had been given for his sixth birthday. It had been rescued from an attic in a state of some disrepair and beautifully restored by the men in the concentration camp who were known in the house as "Vati's workers".

14

The summer before Dieter went into the ack-ack, he had gained a foretaste of what war would not be like. At sixteen, he was packed off to a *Wehrertüchtigungslager* (military training competency camp) for a three-week stay and was loaned the family camera to capture his army exploits. The six teenagers in their barrack hut engaged in horseplay. Dieter snapped one boy with his trousers down, another sleepyhead was caught standing outside still in his dressing gown. Two boys stopped to light a cigarette when they should have been in the heat of battle and the whole team gave mock expressions of sworn loyalty to their Luftwaffe trainer with hands on hearts. The officer in charge of the naïve youths smiled indulgently.

When Dieter did make it to the gun emplacement of Flakgruppe Berlin-West in nearby Dahlem that was to be his working environment for the next eighteen months, he was, in all probability, assigned the role of loader in a team of eleven men and boys. Russian POWs were given the backbreaking role of carrying up the shells from an underground store. An experienced artilleryman, Lieutenant-Colonel König, acted as gun commander and Dieter, his best friend and another *Flakhelfer* had the job of setting fuses and aiming the weapons. The big 88mm guns would fire fifteen shells a minute.

For quite some time, there was very little for them to do. All through the spring and summer of 1943 there was a lull before an explosive storm. The RAF was all this time building squadrons of its new giant bomber, the Avro Lancaster. Arthur "Bomber" Harris was planning an intensive campaign targeting Berlin. "It will cost us between 400 and 500 aircraft. It will cost Germany the war," he boasted.

The heavy raids began in late November and continued right through until the end of March 1944. Several hundred aircraft came each time. They laid waste to nearly half a million homes. The United States Air Force joined the attacks in March, bombing by day. The flak soldiers were suffering from chronic sleep deprivation. On average, Berlin's gun emplacements shot down five bombers each during that four-month period. Given all the burning buildings around, it must have seemed to the men on the ground that they were firing pea-shooters in vain.

The psychological pressures on the exhausted young flak soldiers were enormous. Some suffered nervous breakdowns. The bombers came, on average, every other day. For Dieter, the strain began to show in an incident during the summer of 1944. He returned from a night on duty to an empty house and rooted around in the bottom of a cupboard in the cellar. He pulled out and loaded up the specially engraved rifle that the government had given Karl for his 50th birthday. Then, completely out of character, he went into the garden and started firing it at random.

The neighbours were up in arms and complained afterwards to his parents that this was a peace-loving estate. What was their son doing firing a gun here? When his mother reported back to the family, Dieter, by now almost reckless, fired back: "They make guns to shoot people. What is wrong with what I am doing?"

Breaking point for Dieter came when a bomb scored a direct

hit on his gun emplacement. After the explosion, he looked round to find the headless body of his fellow soldier, former classmate and best friend lying on the ground. "That's it," he told his mother when he returned home. "If they are going to shoot at me, then I am going to shoot back. I'm not just going to sit here waiting for them to come."

There were good reasons for joining the Panzers; and a better one for not doing so. Tank crews had a certain aura in the public eye. They had been portrayed as central figures in the propaganda war played out in the cinema. Films captured victorious tanks thundering through conquered lands, the commander standing triumphant in his turret, the master of his metal chariot. A training circular described them as "the modern equivalent of the cavalry". These dashing men in black were meant to wear their irresistibly glamorous uniforms only on official duty, but they disobeyed the loose order with impunity, walking out as paragons of style in public.

There was one very big downside. Panzer divisions suffered extremely high losses. A direct hit on a tank almost always wiped out the whole crew. By late 1944, signing up for the Panzers was almost as good as signing your own death sentence. Dieter joined the Panzers.

The sole reason he gave for doing so was horribly simple. He told his mother: "I'm not walking." He wanted a company vehicle. It seemed an insane, random decision. It certainly did to Minna. But perhaps Dieter had already seen enough of an insanely random war. If he didn't fancy life as a footslogging infantryman, then joining the Panzers on the basis of a single, sensible conclusion was, in his view, as good a reason as any.

Dieter did not become part of a Panzer unit in the ordinary Wehrmacht. The son of an SS officer, he joined its military wing, the Waffen SS. Whether this was out of conviction or convenience is unknown. The political beliefs at that time of the boy who had been steeped in Nazi philosophy through school from the age of seven and the Hitler Youth for nearly eight years can only be imagined.

An immensely proud father took his son to training school, as if he were taking his child to his first day at university. They arrived at the gates of Neuruppin, a giant complex of three-storey buildings a short distance north of Berlin. Karl wore his best SS uniform, Dieter his blue-black Hitler Youth outfit and little peaked cap. On 23rd November 1944, Dieter was enrolled in the 5th Panzer Replacement Battalion. Very soon after, he boarded a train to a Panzer training school in Sagan (Zagan in present-day Poland), north-east of Dresden.

Dieter underwent only the most rudimentary training. Earlier in the war, a member of a tank crew would have expected to be training for over a year before he was ready to fight. He would have had four and a half months of basic training, learning routine drill and how to use pistols, rifles and machine guns. He would have had two and a half months working in a tank with his close-knit team of five. He would have spent several months more taking part in combat training – driving the tank over the heaths of Sagan with live ammunition landing all around. By the end of 1944, things were different. Dieter would be thrown into battle after four months.

15

For the children, Christmas 1944 was magical, just like the ones they used to know. The grown-ups had strung up a full-length curtain to act as a screen between the dining room and the living room. Eki tried to peek round and was "persuaded" not to. Out of sight, behind the curtain, was an enormous Christmas tree almost the height of the room, the biggest they had ever had. Karl and Minna were putting up the decorations on the tree – baubles, stars, lead tinsel that hung straight and proper candles that were lit up.

At the appointed hour, Karl rang a bell on the tree and the curtain was drawn back for the family to see the adorned tree. Everyone was given a cardboard plate embossed with a Christmas emblem. Most amazing of all in a nation at war, there were biscuits on the plates: "We *never* had biscuits!" exclaimed Rudi. The boys had presents too. Eki was given a Dornier model aircraft. Rudi sat at the dining-room table and buried his head in a new book.

It was a special treat for the family to have Dieter home on Christmas leave. He returned from training school in his black Panzer uniform, a sinister death's head motif on each collar. But he must have been like a student on his first trip home from university. Half of him was there with his family; the other half was lost in his head with his new family of army comrades. His stay was all too brief; his mother's grief at his departure can only be imagined.

Where Dieter went at the end of the Christmas break is not certain. If he returned to Sagan to resume training, it would have been a short stay. There was deep snow and the temperature was 20 degrees centigrade below zero. Worse still, the Russian army was approaching. At the end of the month, the town was taken. It is more likely that Dieter was posted south in the new year to Erlangen, a Panzer training camp in – at that time – safe Bavaria.

For the family left behind, January was a month of relentless bad news. A last big push on the Western Front to drive the Allies back had been repulsed. Worse still, the Soviet advance from the east accelerated towards the capital. Stories filtered back and were magnified by Goebbels' propaganda machine, of atrocities committed by Russian soldiers on civilians, of wholesale murder, rape and mutilation. Dark humour played out in the streets of Berlin. The ubiquitous LSR signs that stood for *Luftschützraum* (air raid shelter) were now said to mean *Lernt Russisch Schnell* (learn Russian quickly).

Within Dienstweg 19, Rudi could feel the fear. He was told stories that circulated around Karl's office, or were passed by word of mouth around the SS estate: "They said the Russians had no civilisation whatsoever. We heard that when they took over a town they didn't know what the toilet was for so they used it to wash their potatoes. They said they were a cruel people: that was their nature."

The family maid decided not to hang around to find out. One day, Grete simply disappeared, taking all the Niemanns' bed linen with her.

There were signs of imminent collapse in the city. Refugees were pouring into Berlin from the east at the rate of 50,000 a day. The government ordered anti-tank trenches to be dug around the city.

Air raids intensified with a thousand bombers at a time coming every day for 56 consecutive days. Shortages became more acute. A new film called *Kolberg*, the epic of epics involving tens of thousands of Wehrmacht soldiers as extras, was released, but scarcely anyone saw it – virtually all of Berlin's cinemas had been bombed or were closed because of coal shortages.

Minna could no longer contain her antipathy towards the regime. She began to speak out, loudly. Rudi witnessed her clashes with Karl: "He was telling her to keep her voice down, keep quiet." Anne was in touch with Dieter in Bavaria by now and raised her concerns about her mother's outspoken comments. And not without reason, for by now the state had turned on its own people. On 9th March, Hitler established flying courts martial, whose job was to hunt down those accused of undermining the war effort. Trials were perfunctory; the sentence was always death. And the family was living in an estate full of zealots who might be more ready to denounce than ordinary Berliners.

The adults began to suspect that it wasn't just the walls that had ears. They answered the phone: "Berlin-Zehlendorf 858482?" and heard odd clicks and crackles on the line. They believed their phone was being tapped. In their fearful minds, the Gestapo was just a rap at the door away. Minna wrote a letter to Bavaria, asking Dieter what they should do.

Hide. And Seek.

16

The corridors of the SS empire were that bit emptier when Karl returned to work after Christmas 1944. The offices that, altogether, had thronged with more than 1,500 workers, now had little more than a third of that number. All of the women workers were laid off for the new year: almost all of the men of fighting age had gone to the front. Though Karl never joined the Volkssturm, Hitler's Dad's Army, he had kept a parallel role in the rank of *Hauptsturmführer* in the Waffen SS, since 1942, when he had transferred from the ordinary Wehrmacht. The tubby, distinctly sedentary man approaching his 52nd birthday was hardly primed for action. He stayed at his desk.

What exactly was he able to do? Although 1944 had brought the "workforce" in the concentration camps up to 50,000, as the German army emptied Hungary and other eastern occupied countries of their Jewish populations, Karl's woodworking factories were rendered almost irrelevant by the wholesale deployment of inmates in private companies making munitions, such as Messerschmitt and Heinkel, as well as sub-camps doing likewise, in particular Mittelbau-Dora, the Buchenwald sub-camps where 60,000 slave labourers toiled to make weapons and died in abominable conditions. For the Nazis, labour was cheap, plentiful and disposable.

One by one, Karl's factories were being subjected to Allied take-overs. The eastern camps that had contributed more than half of all production were gone. Lublin had been liberated by the Russian army the previous July. Auschwitz and Stutthof followed in January. That same month, Sachsenhausen reported mounting difficulties in obtaining materials – targeted Allied bombing of railway lines had disrupted transport links.

For too long, Karl's überbosses were lost in dreams. Well into 1944, Himmler and Pohl still believed that the shift of emphasis towards armaments production was a temporary blip. There would be a time when they could switch back to furnishing the empire in the east, even though by now there was no east to furnish. One of Oswald Pohl's deputies shored up his leader's delusions, writing: "The economic enterprises of the SS were not established for the purposes of a speedy recovery, but for ever."

By 1945, reality had dawned. Every SS officer must have known full well that if they were captured by the Russians they – and probably their families too – would be summarily killed. Karl had received Himmler's order of 21st January, stating that anyone leaving his position in any military or civilian office without being ordered to do so would be punished with death. Karl sat at his desk, managing a dwindling workforce and waited for instructions.

Soon, Berlin would be left to old men, women, children and half a million Russian soldiers. The SS ran away. At the end of March, Karl was given the instruction that he would be part of be a strategic redeployment, an office move to southern Germany. Until things were back to normal.

Though he would have no factories and no workers, Karl may have believed in the fiction of relocation. At the very least, he would have had his self-esteem bolstered by the knowledge that he was merely following orders. Karl's boss, Josef Opperbeck, was part of a contingent who burned plenty of documents, then loaded essential office files into vehicles and headed for Bavaria. Much later, Oswald Pohl would go south too, before disappearing under a false name and with forged papers.

Others made a less dignified exit. Neighbours of Karl Bestle observed that, latterly, the officer who had been so full of bluff and bravado in their presence had become a very anxious man. He even began to express criticism of the party he had backed for more than twenty years. Bestle did not wait for orders: in those last weeks of war, he fled the city towards safe anonymity in a town near the Danish border.

17

"This is a silly damn way to fight a war. We just go out and chase the Krauts off that hill and then come on back. We could have them halfway to Berlin if we kept on going." Nevertheless, the disgruntled American soldier went out on patrol once again, stealing through mountainous, heavily forested country – the most rugged terrain on the Western Front – in snow and cold rain, on the alert for mines that would blow a leg off, and enemy troops, waiting just a few hundred yards to the east.

Just six months before, the US 42nd "Rainbow" Infantry Division, containing men from all 48 states, had been training for battle in sun-kissed Oklahoma. Their preparations were cut short in December 1944, when they were called to battle in France. Their job was to boost Allied efforts to repulse *Operation Nordwind*, the German army's final big offensive of the war. The infantrymen joined a task force in forested Alsace-Lorraine and began fighting on the last day of 1944.

By the middle of February, the whole division had pushed through the mountains until they were close to the German border. But while they had vastly superior numbers and weaponry, they were facing crack troops of the 6th Gebirgsjäger – a mountain division with more than four years of experience in such testing conditions. The US army paused, sending out reconnaissance parties to assess strengths and weaknesses in the German line.

At the end of the month, the expert but exhausted German mountain division was relieved by a less experienced grenadier regiment. The new recruits to the front were, in the words of one US officer, "old men and young boys". They must have been daunted by the opposition. A US patrol captured one rookie German soldier, who asked fearfully: "Is your division a part of Roosevelt's SS?"

Meanwhile, Dieter's reservist unit was posted – not to the Russian front, as they had all expected – but to the Panzer training grounds in the north Bavarian town of Erlangen. Here, they began practising for the battle to come. During breaks, the men were able to write home. At this stage of the war they were writing without any fear of their letters being censored. And so they could put down their private thoughts and aspirations. It is astonishing that even in the late, chaotic stages of the war, letters were still getting through, transported from one end of Germany to the other. Only four of Dieter's letters survive, scrawled in pencil in near illegible script:

Erlangen, 8.III.45

Dear Dad,

You will be surprised, but I want to write to you too. Hereby I would like to personally thank you for the cigarettes, and both of the letters. I was absolutely delighted, as this happens very rarely; I don't want to complain – you have much work to do and things to worry about, so you don't have the time to write. When the son writes he always asks for favours. It is terrible. Anna-Luise wrote to me that Mum has started on a political trial of strength again. I have sent a letter to Mum. Hopefully, it will calm her down. I don't want her to do anything stupid because of this. Please talk again to her. I hope that time will soon convince Mum.

Now here comes just one more request. I have here my address, would you please ask if the publisher can still deliver those books? Would you get them for me? Rudi* and his wife could also use them.

For today that's enough

I greet and kiss you all.
Your Dieter

For the education and training of officers Publisher E.S. Mittler and Sons, Berlin SW 68

1) Officers' Topics	2.50
2) Lance Sergeants' Topics	2.50
3) Captains' Notebook	1.00
4) Small bearings and their implementation	2.00
5) MG 34†	.60
6) Tasks for Platoon and Company	2.50
7) Shooting Training	2.00
8) Shooting in the Infantry	1.20
9) Topography	6.75
10) Tank Troops and the Operation of Heavy Weaponry	1.80
11) Gas Weapons, and Defence	5.80
12) Guidelines for Tank Gunners	
13) The Sergeant	2.00

Not only does the letter show the boy's concern about what might happen to his mother for voicing unguarded, outspoken views, but

---

* Clearly not his 11-year-old brother!

† Maschinengewehr 34, a type of machine gun.

he is also anxious to patch up the gaps in his military education, seeking in the manuals he requests what he has missed in hopelessly foreshortened training.

Exactly a week after Dieter wrote home, the Rainbow Division mounted a full-scale assault on the German defences in Alsace-Lorraine. Three days later, they crossed the German border. They reached the heavily fortified Siegfried Line. Concrete pillboxes were impressive defences, but not when they were manned by soldiers who fled in disorderly retreat.

The division reached the German town of Dahn and paused for a rest. Many of the troops celebrated Passover, the most significant event in the Jewish calendar, celebrating the liberation of Moses' people from captivity. The significance could not be understated on that wet and wintry morning. The Jewish chaplain requisitioned the town hall and held a service of thanksgiving. Soldiers spilled out into the streets outside. The townspeople stood around them and watched.

On the same day, Dieter wrote a hurried letter home that leaps confusingly from subject to subject, but nevertheless reveals in its haste the thoughts that were uppermost in his mind:

Erlangen (local accommodation) 22.III.45

Dear parents, and siblings,

Now, that the post probably takes even longer to arrive than before, I want to get some lines ready quickly, because the postal service truck is coming soon.

*I have not received any mail from you for several days. But I have not given up hope yet. Right now, there is a break for me in training. The weather has become horrible and dreary. It is great**

---

* The original German word "*toll*" indicates that Dieter is being heavily ironic.

what our enemies to the west are smug about, but our defence measures will soon show them that the sun will not shine on them every day. Their losses will ensure that. The clowns should not think that they can just walk about in Germany whenever they want to. That can't be. "Amen to that." On Sunday the sun will be shining in the sky for us.

Guess what I had last night for dinner? Fried potatoes with bacon, and a fried egg on top. That was a delicacy. Everything was organised, and it was free. On Sunday, between 10 and 11am, I had a hearty farmer's breakfast: bread, butter, bacon and sausage. It was delicious.

Oh, how silly and stupid I used to be. I hope I receive mail today. You are still healthy, aren't you? I can say the same of me. May we soon see each other again, in the time of victory.

I greet and kiss you all
Your Dieter

The boy who had left Berlin as a vegetarian had turned into an enthusiastic carnivore. And the last line betrays his political standpoint. Dieter's sign-off line in German was *"Wiedersehen im Sieg"* (see you again in the time of victory). It is classic Nazi phraseology.

Three days later, another snatched letter, another hasty tumult of thoughts:

Erlangen, 25.III.45

Dear parents, and siblings,

Now that I have half an hour off, I would like to quickly take the chance to send you some lines. Thanks again, I was delighted about

Above: Officer cadet Karl Niemann, August 1914 (p.253, no.1)
Below: Newly-weds Minna and Karl, c1921 (p.253, no.2)

Above: Minna wearing Karl's army tunic c1916 (p.254, no.3)
Below: Anne and Dieter, Summer c1930 (p.254, no.4)
Right: Anne and Dieter, Dortmund, Christmas 1928 (p.254, no.5)

Above: Army parade, Dortmund, early 1930s (p. 254, no. 6)
Below: Stormtrooper rally, Dortmund, c1930 (p. 254, no. 7)

Left: Anne in League of German Girls (BDM) uniform, c1936 (p.255, no.8)

Below: Karl wearing Nazi Party and SS pin badges, February 1940 (p.255, no.9)

Below: Arrival of senior SS officer at Dachau Concentration Camp, 1935/6 (p.255, no.10)

Above: SS social outing, Bavaria, c1937 (p.256, no.12)
Left: Karl in Nazi Party uniform, Dortmund, 1933 (p.256, no.11)
Below: The Nazi Party! New Year celebrations, Berlin, 1939 (p.257, no.13)

Above: Karl and Eki, Berlin, 1938/9 (p.257, no.14)
Below: Father and son, Berlin, 1938/9 (p.257, no.15)

Above: Minna, Rudi and Eki, c1943 (p.258, no.16)
Below: Family and friends, summer 1939 (p.258, no.17)

Right: Eki with the family silver,
1944 (p.258, no.19)

Left: Minna and Dieter, c1942
(p.258, no.18)

Below: The family bunker, Berlin,
1944 (p.259, no.20)

Above: First day at Panzer school, November 1944 (p.259, no.21)
Below: Military training camp, 1942 (p.259, no.22)

Above: Dieter in uniform (with SS flashes obliterated), 1945 (p. 259, no. 23)
Below: The same picture with SS flashes digitally restored

Above: Rudi and Eki fraternising with the enemy, Spring 1945 (p.260, no.24)

Below: Downtime at Anne's wedding, Hameln, 1947 (p.260, no.25)

Above: The Niemann family, Hameln, 1950 (p. 260, no. 26)
Below: Minna, Karl and mysterious friend, Hameln, 1959 (p. 261, no. 27)

Above: Rudi's family, Glasgow, 1963, the author with teddy bear (p.261, no.28)

Below: Three little braves, Glasgow, 1965 (p.261, no.29)

it [presumably a letter they had sent], the postal service is terribly irregular. I am, apart from toothache, still satisfactorily healthy. I hope to hear the same about you.

Now I want to reply to Mum's letter. As for the wiretapping from Berlin, I can't give advice. They can only do that when one is charged with a crime. You write, dear Mum, that I probably forgot the birthday. I know that is definitely not the case. Did you not receive my birthday letter? I sent the letter 10 days in advance, so that it would arrive on time. Once in a while we go to Nuremberg to do work-related tasks, among other things. It is also incredibly hot right now. One starts sweating when one just sits around.

Please give Horst Gleiss my best wishes to get better soon. Also, please thank Frau Finger from me for the smoking stamps. I was very happy that my dear neighbours have not forgotten about me (…).

At the front, things will soon turn back in our favour again, then the other side will well and truly run. Next winter, the food rationing will probably be better. This year the war will come to an end, the result will be decided. Both sides have reached the peak of their power, whoever has the greater reserves for the last five minutes will win the war. There is a lot of work for us again. It is terrible in that regard. I hope you are all safe and sound.

I greet and kiss you all
Your Dieter

Dieter was insistent he had not forgotten matters of great importance in Berlin. It had been Rudi's birthday on the 17th. And yes, he had remembered. There was also the small matter of the family phone being bugged.

In Bavaria, his unit had been taken a few miles south to Nuremberg. Most likely the work-related tasks that he speaks about were clearing up bomb damage. Approximately one million bombs were dropped on the city on 2nd January and further air raids took place on 20th and 21st February.

Out to the west, US Lieutenant Hugh C. Daly wrote: "Trucks and tanks and jeeps had been pouring over the Rhine bridges at Worms in a never-ending stream for three days. Truck after truck and convoy after convoy roared through tiny German villages all day and all night." This may have been the trigger for what happened next. The Rainbow Division was striking out north-east towards the city of Würzburg. The German High Command may have decided that this was the point to bring in all available reserves to meet the enemy in battle.

Erlangen, 28.III.45

Dear parents and siblings,

We have arrived at the station in the freight wagons. There you go. They need us at the front. So that's me done with high school.

This time it's the same as in Sagan,* with the only difference that it's not against Russia but against the west. It is better in many respects that it's against the west.

Hopefully you are all well. I can certainly say that of myself. Who would have thought such a thing on Sunday? Keep writing to the old address until I tell you a new one. Always inform xxxxx [illegible] and xxxxxx [illegible] of the latest. If the connection should not work for some reason, I will get myself back there somehow. So you'll always get the latest.

I will always think of you. Just as before. When it comes to a fight, I will always fight thinking of you at home. Then it is easier. Then

---

* Dieter's Panzer training school.

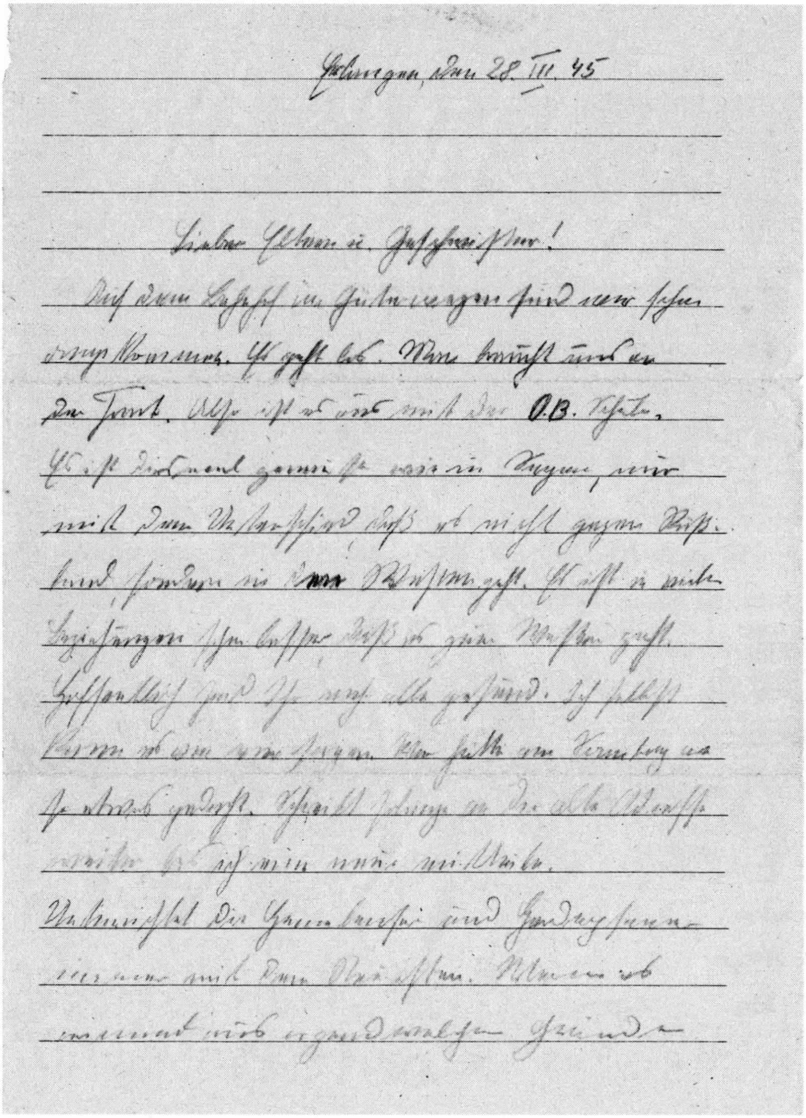

Erlangen, den 28. III. 45

Liebe Eltern u. Geschwister!

[Handwritten letter in German Kurrent script, largely illegible.]

Feldpost

Familie
Karl Niemann
Berlin - Zehlendorf
Dienstweg 19

ERLANGEN
29.3.45 11-12

Abs.: A. Schr. Niemann
3/0.B. Schule L13 a) Erlangen
Pz. Kaserne 4 Komp.

you know what you are fighting for. I will always fight to be true to my promise.

In the hope of peace soon, things are easier to bear. Now you don't need to give a letter/little parcel to xxxxxxx [illegible]. In the course of the night or early in the morning things will happen.

I greet and kiss you all.
Your Dieter

Greetings to all my friends

A week after writing this letter, Dieter was dead. It is possible, to some extent, to follow the last days of his life. A train undoubtedly took him somewhere in the vicinity of Würzburg, a once elegant city that had been bombed to rubble in under twenty minutes a fortnight before, with 5,000 of its citizens killed in the resulting firestorm. Someone had painted "*Heil Hitler*" in white graffiti on the walls of the roofless fortress overlooking the river Main. The remnant of the German army retreating from the French border had halted to make a last stand among the ruins. Dieter's unit may well have joined them there.

On the morning of 4th April, American foot soldiers poured over a bridgehead on the Main. Lieutenant Daly wrote:

Now the Rainbow met what was perhaps the most bitter resistance encountered while it was fighting as a complete unit. Civilians joined military personnel in battling the attackers. City firemen and policemen joined in the defense of the city. Nearly every house and building contained snipers and panzerfausts were lobbed like mortars into our lines. Beneath the city streets were networks of*

* Hand-held anti-tank grenade launchers.

underground tunnels and the defenders retreated into these and then came up behind the Rainbowmen and attacked them from the rear.

Tanks would have had extremely limited manoeuvrability in the debris-strewn, narrow streets. And the indications are that there was no more than a handful left in the whole German force. It is more than possible that Dieter never actually fought in a tank, but went into battle on foot.

Some time on that same day of heavy fighting, Dieter was badly wounded. He did not die on a pile of broken bricks in the city, but was borne away alive from the fighting. The family would one day be told that he was taken to a hospital. The likelihood is that he was carried by his own side away from the battle, along with a number of other wounded Germans. They were taken to a field hospital, a tented medical facility in the hamlet of Iffigheim, ten miles south-west of the city. On the night of 4th April, or on the day after, Dieter died. He was nineteen years old and the end of the war was 33 days away.

The US Division Narrative and Statistics reported: "After 3 days of difficult bloody fighting against fanatical resistance, the Rainbow cleared the skeleton city of WURZBURG on 5th April 1945."

18

One evening towards the end of March 1945, Karl came home from work to tell the family that his office was being relocated. They would be travelling to a place called Spitzingsee in the Alps, and three of his colleagues and their families would be going with them. The children were thrilled at the prospect of a big adventure and an exciting-sounding destination. On the following day, Minna began to get things organised. She packed clothes, linen and things of value, such as the little case containing the family silver that Eki had so diligently carried to the bunker every night and day.

Minna went to elaborate lengths, even wrapping up Dieter's confirmation suit and folding it carefully away. It may have represented an intimate association with her absent son. It might also have offered a promise, that her younger sons would one day wear it for their own confirmations when life returned to normality.

Karl returned that night and saw the extent of his wife's preparations. He put his hands up to his face: "For heaven's sake, what's this all about? We will be back in Berlin in four weeks' time."

With hindsight, it seems an astonishing outburst. In the west, the Allies had crossed the Rhine, the last natural barrier to the invading forces. In the east, the advancing Russians had reached

East Prussia. The Reich's secret weapons, the V2 rockets that had promised to reverse their fortunes, had had little impact and every rocket base but one was now in Allied hands. All around, Germany was tumbling to defeat, yet it appeared Karl was still unaware, still believing in *Endsieg*, the final victory. Or maybe he was putting on a brave face to cheer up his family. Minna said nothing in reply to his remonstration, and nor did she unpack any of their belongings afterwards.

Early on an April morning, before the American bombers arrived for their daily pounding of the city, the Niemanns and the other SS families set off together. They passed through bomb-shattered suburbs. In less than three weeks' time, boys as young as Rudi would be fighting Russian soldiers here. The families travelled in a small convoy of trucks and cars. There was no petrol available, so the vehicles had been modified to run on wood. The adults got into the cars, and the children climbed into trucks that each had a wooden burner, a boiler at the back and a cylinder to feed gases into the engine. The vehicles worked well enough on the straight, but they puttered and spluttered every time they toiled up a hill. And the stink lingered in the boys' nostrils long after the vehicles had come to rest.

It was an uncomfortable ride in more than one respect. The families were driving through a narrow corridor between Allied forces which were closing in from both east and west. The danger of attack from low-flying enemy aircraft was very real. Even so, the calls of nature required that they had to stop every so often, and besides, the drivers needed rests.

On one of these comfort breaks, Eki spotted a meadow beside the road full of early-spring flowers and had a truly wonderful idea. He decided that he would pick a bunch for his mother. Unnoticed by the others, he slipped off the road, wandered down into the field and became lost in his thoughts, as he plucked the best blooms. The rest of the travellers boarded their vehicles again and the convoy set off, failing to realise that one of their number had been left behind.

A few minutes down the road, Minna began to feel uneasy. She asked if her youngest child was definitely on board one of the trucks. Her companions in the car assured her that he must certainly be there, but the anxious mother was unconvinced. She put her foot down and the driver put his on the brake. The whole convoy came to a stop and then it was discovered that the child was missing. Eki recalled:

> One car drove back to the rest place. There I stood – knowing and understanding nothing of the confusion of war – very happy with a bunch of flowers in my hands – and I could not understand what all the excitement was about. I was just proud of the bouquet of flowers I had for Mum and I had no idea whatsoever about the danger around me, around us, from enemy aircraft. How should I as a young child have understood that?

The families carried on southwards on a slow journey of about 350 miles, stopping for the night and sleeping in their vehicles. Minna was growing increasingly irritated with one particularly fanatical Nazi family among them, who rose the following morning and ritually gave everyone else in the entourage "the German greeting" – the Nazi salute of "*Heil Hitler!*" The parents had three children, named in a typically conformist Nazi style that often used rhyme or alliteration: Heike, Anke, Elke.* The mother was pregnant and

---

* With more than a nod of homage to Hitler, Joseph and Magda Goebbels had named their children Hedwig, Helga, Holdine, Hildegaard, Helmut and Heidrun.

Minna remarked with heavy sarcasm that the child would probably be called Wibke to complete a rhyming quartet.

The column of vehicles entered northern Bavaria and passed just 30 miles from Dieter's last known address. The sounds of heavy artillery could be heard too, because the battle frontline in the west was the same distance away.

On 8th April, the convoy arrived on the outskirts of Dachau at a distinctly odd road sign. Three running soldiers made out of wood, the leader blowing a bugle, were mounted on a direction arrow that pointed left to the SS training camp. On top of the direction arrow pointing right, a burly SS guard was depicted goading two figures, stereotypical sinister Jews with huge noses and dark-rimmed eyes.

The cars and trucks had reached the gates of an overfilled hell. For the best part of ten years, Karl had very carefully kept his work life separate from his home. Now he was bringing his home to work. Karl had worked at Dachau for three years, but the concentration camp to which he returned that April was a very different proposition from the one he had inspected from time to time during the war years.

In the previous few weeks, Natzweiler, Buchenwald and Flossenbürg had been evacuated, bringing train transports carrying more than 20,000 prisoners to Dachau, and one by one, the sub-camps closed too, driving thousands more inside the main camp. The same rations were meant to feed the extra starving mouths, the same insanitary conditions were endured in an institution which had been built to accommodate 20,000 inmates, but now had more than three times that number. Thousands had died in an outbreak of typhus in November. Another epidemic was about to break out. Bodies had been taken out of the camp to be buried on a nearby hill. Very soon, the guards would give up bothering to have them moved and would simply order men to pile the corpses of their fellow prisoners up in the open. At the time of the convoy's arrival, the authorities were busily plotting *Wolke AI* (Cloud AI) and *Wolkenbrand* (Cloud fire), code names for plans to kill all of the inmates.

As in 1935, Karl did not enter the concentration camp itself, but went left, taking his party through the entrance of the much bigger SS complex on the other side of the wire. The boys were thrilled when they were taken into a barrack hut and given bunk beds. The *Totenkopfverbände* (death's head guards) had slept there before them, men who had been trained to bully, abuse and murder. The family was housed within sight of a low brick building partially obscured by trees. It had an unusually tall chimney.

Restless after the confinement of their long journey, the boys went out to play. They found a broken-down Sanka, an ambulance van, which had been left on the road with the key still in the ignition. Rudi got into the driver's seat and made as if he knew how to drive the fuel-less vehicle. It was enough to convince Eki, who bounced about in the passenger seat, proud to be sitting next to his so capable and grown-up brother.

In the barrack hut, Minna felt the loss of something she had forgotten to pack for the journey. The family were lacking the small wooden boards that they used as plates to take *Abendbrot* – suppers of bread, meat and cheese. The order went through to the camp and, at some point during the family's stay, inmates were tasked with making a platter for each of them. Karl may have gone into the workshop to supervise; he may have gone into the offices too and found prisoner Karl Steiner, the man he had tried and failed to release nearly three years before, still working at his desk.

Karl Niemann's SS colleagues in the camp were engaged in something far less innocent. While Karl's party halted at Dachau for two or three nights, enough time for the vehicles to be filled with wood, and food supplies packed for their occupants, other dirty work was going on. During the family's stay there, someone dug a wide trench about a foot deep, filled it with enormous quantities of paper and set light to it, creating a giant bonfire. The SS were disposing of all potentially incriminating evidence before the Allies reached the camp, and, in all probability, a group of inmates was given the job beforehand of digging a pit as an incinerator.

For the second time within a matter of days, Eki went wandering off on his own. He made his way through a maze of low huts towards the entrance of the training camp. Some instinct made him enter one of the huts. The smell hit him instantly. Not the stink of disease, death and decay that wafted across from the camp over the fence. In this high-ceilinged hut were sweet, fragrant perfumes of pine, larch, oak and beech. Quite by chance, Eki had stumbled into the carpenters' workshop.

Within a week, all work would stop at Dachau. The daily processions to the workshops of those prisoners who could still stand would cease. But when Eki walked into the *Tischlerei*, there were men standing at the benches. They wore the striped uniforms that Eki knew well as workers' clothes, the same uniforms that men had worn when they came to do odd jobs at his father's house, and so he had no reason to be afraid. He wandered from bench to bench, sniffing the pine-scented air, and marvelling at all the different machines. The men must have looked down and wondered who this dark-haired child was and what he was doing there. The little boy, the son of the SS officer who had overall control of the workshops, wandered entranced among them. They carried on working, plying their sharp saws and heavy hammers.

A hastily convened search party entered the building and found the lost child. Eki was gathered up with some alacrity and whisked back to the bosom of his family.

The following day, a man was murdered just a few metres from where the Niemanns slept. His name was Georg Elser. A carpenter, communist and devoted churchgoer, 42-year-old Elser had been a long-term opponent of the Nazi regime. In November 1939, he had single-handedly carried out a plot to kill Hitler in Munich's Bürgerbräukeller on the anniversary of the Beer Hall Putsch, Hitler's failed snatch at power in 1923. The bomb he had planted in a pillar of the room exploded, but Hitler had given his speech thirteen minutes earlier than planned and had already left the building. For five and a half years, Elser had been held, first in Sachsenhausen, then in Dachau, as a special security prisoner, for the Gestapo suspected he could not have operated alone and the plan had always been to have a show trial to display him as part of a British plot. But with the war as good as lost, Hitler sent orders from Berlin. Elser was taken behind the brick building facing the Niemanns' barrack hut and shot.

It was a lovely spring day and the boys decided to go outside and play hide-and-seek. It was Eki's turn to hide. He went to the edge of a pit full of ashes – the pit that had been dug the day before – and had an ingenious thought. He would bury himself completely. He jumped into the trench, through the white ashes on the surface and into the still-glowing embers underneath. Nearly 70 years later, Eki still had bare patches on his calves where no hair would grow. The little boy cried out in fear and pain, sounds that summoned adults to pull him out and tend to his burned legs.

Now the family really were confined to barracks. Eki lay on his bunk, his injured limbs bandaged. Rudi sat bored in the corner of a room close to his mother and father. The two adults were talking, scarcely aware of their son's presence. He remembered that he looked out of the window to see what his parents were staring at. He saw dark smoke rising from the tall chimney of the brick building opposite.

"You know what they're doing there?" said Minna. "You know what they're doing to the Jews?"

"No," said Karl. "What?"

"They're killing them. They're killing them and they're burning the bodies," said Minna.

"No, no, they wouldn't do that," said Karl.

"Yes, they would," insisted Minna. "Can't you smell it? Can't you smell the flesh?"

The conversation, remembered by Rudi for the rest of his life, says much about both of his parents. The crematorium – for that is what the building was – had been constructed in 1942. But though there was smoke that day, this was fire of a different sort. The camp had run out of coal in February 1945; the prisoners who died after then were no longer cremated. Minna could not smell burning bodies, but most likely putrefying corpses over the fence. Nevertheless, the exchange gives compelling evidence that she knew something of the Final Solution, that news had filtered through to the housewives within the SS enclave of Zehlendorf about what was really happening to the Jews. And so she was able to make, as it turned out, an erroneous assumption.

That single exchange between husband and wife suggests very strongly that, for all the closeness of their relationship, there was a great gulf in communication that neither would attempt to bridge. As long as they had been in Berlin, Minna had not dared ask certain questions for fear of the answers she might receive.

19

Exactly three weeks after the Niemann family entered Dachau, some other visitors arrived at the camp. Battle-weary soldiers of the US Seventh Army had ridden their jeeps into the town unopposed early in the day. They included men of the 42nd Rainbow Infantry Division, the same soldiers who had wiped out Dieter's Panzer unit only a few weeks before.

In the railway siding close to the camp, they found a train of abandoned cattle trucks, full of the bodies of prisoners who had been transferred from Buchenwald. Those who had not died inside the trucks on the journey had been shot as soon as the doors were opened. The US soldiers pressed on to the camp itself, where they were met with sniper fire from a handful of SS guards who were holding out inside. One by one, the snipers were picked off.

There were more horrors awaiting the soldiers when they were welcomed through the gates of the camp late in the afternoon by other German officers and guards wishing to appease and placate the victors. They found yet more bodies – 3,000 of them crammed in the rooms of the crematorium and piled up in heaps outside. Some of the soldiers, enraged by the deprivation and suffering they found among the emaciated inmates, carried out summary reprisals on their torturers, lining guards up against a wall and shooting them, or handing them over to the inmates who beat the most sadistic of their oppressors to death with spades, shovels, or shot them with pistols that were passed to them for the deed. Typhus was rife in the camp and liberation came too late for more than 3,000 of the inmates, who were to die in the following days.

The four SS families missed all of this, for they had already gone. A Dachau official had faithfully recorded the Niemann family's arrival in town on 8th April, by typing their details out on a card. Every German was required, by law, to provide information to the relevant authorities about their place of abode at all times; when they arrived, where they had lived before, and where exactly they were going next. Curiously enough, the hitherto law-abiding Niemanns broke the rules by leaving no record of their destination. For the sake of completeness, the Dachau official noted under the column "Departed to", "Unknown after 26.4.45".

The SS entourage had set off on the morning of 11th April, the vehicles stocked up with fresh supplies of wood and food. They pressed on south, beyond Munich and towards the snowy peaks of the Alps. The trucks and jeeps reached the foothills, passed the railhead at the lakeside town of Schliersee, then cut off up a narrow, steep road, winding through dark conifer forests where melting snow had turned mountain streams into gushing torrents.

Karl knew the way. He had been up this mountain road four years earlier, for at that time, the tiny village of Spitzingsee, 300 metres above the broader valley of Schliersee, contained a sub-camp of Dachau. At least one detachment of inmates had been sent there to assemble mountain huts – wood-framed chalets where SS officers could go on summer retreats. And now here was a group of SS families heading to the hills for the summer and most definitely in retreat.

First card

Familienname und Vorname	Staatsangehörigkeit:	Deutsches Reich							
	Stand und Gewerbe	Geburts- Tag / Monat / Jahr	Geburtsort (Bezirksamt)	Religion	Zugezogen von	am	Weggezogen nach	am
a) **Niemann** **Karl**	SS-Wirt- schaftsprü- fer	3o. 4.93	Hemeringen Kreis am Hameln	gottgl.	Prittlbach 6.3.36		Berlin W 50 Augsburger- str.48 Gartenhaus	15 6 38
led., verh., geschied., verw.							29.8.1938	
b) Ehefrau **Wilhelmina**		28.12.95	Hameln Kreis am Hameln	ev.	Dortmund 6.6.36		Hameln Adolf- str.2	
geborene: **Schwenker**								
c) Kinder							29.8.38	
N.**Annelies** e		1. 11. 23	Hameln	"	"	"	Hameln,Adolf- str.2	
N.**Dieter**		23. 1. 26	"	"	"	"		
N.**Rudolf**		17. 3. 34	Dortmund	"	x"	"	"	
N.**Ekart Wilh.Josef**		6. 1.38	Prittlbach ev.		1938		"	

am 29.1o.37 Austritt aus
der Ev.Rel.Ges.

Second card

Familienname und Vorname	Staatsangehörigkeit:	Deutsches Reich							
	Stand und Gewerbe	Geburts- Tag / Mon. / Jahr	Geburtsort (Landkreis)	Reli- gion	Zugezogen von	am	Weggezogen nach	am
N i e m a n n Karl	SS-Haupt- sturmführer	30.4. 93	Hemeringen	ggl.	Bln.Zehlen- dorf 8.4.45 Prov./Zone		unbekannt verz. 26.4.45 Prov./Zone	
? led., verh., geschied., verw.								
Ehefrau Wilhelmine		28.12.95	Hameln	?	?			
geb.: Schwenker								
Kinder:								
N. Annelies		1.1. 23	Hameln	?				
N. Rudi		17. 3.34	Dortmund	?				
N. Ekart		6.1. 38	Prittelbach	?				

Aufenthalt genehmigt
von   bis

The wood-fired lorries heaved up a last stretch of the mountain pass, then rode down into a hanging valley where there was a blue-green Alpine lake no more than a quarter of a mile across. At the far end was Spitzingsee village, pinpointed by its pointy church spire. The party did not go as far as the church, or in among the dwellings, but halted just short of the settlement at the foot of a track that was knee-deep in snow. The vehicles could not drive up the mountain, and so the families began to unload their belongings. The whole operation had been planned in advance. The Niemanns were given a horse. An old horse. An old, blind horse. It trod on Anne's foot. But the laden beast knew the way and so the family walked along beside it (Anne limping), with their feet becoming soaked in slushy snow, climbing until they reached their accommodation, near the head of the narrow valley.

The *Schwarzenkopfhütte* (black-head hut) at the very end of the track was more a lodge than a cabin, a giant, multi-roomed stone chalet that had, earlier in the war, belonged to the Gebirgsjäger, the army's mountain light infantry. It had lain empty for some time and now the families climbed an outside staircase, then opened doors into a dusty shell. All that the previous occupants had left behind were handbooks about various forms of armed warfare. Rudi and the other children gathered them up and would, over the next few days, amuse themselves by tearing them apart to make paper aeroplanes.

Snow lay deep on the ground behind the lodge on the day they arrived. A little farther back there was a smattering of conifers and then there was nothing – just a sheer drop into the next valley. For the wife and mother who had toiled up the mountain, it must have seemed at that moment as if her husband had brought her to the end of the world. Rudi remembered only one moment in his life when he heard his mother give his father a bitter reproach. This was probably it: "Look where your Mr Hitler has got us now."

Minna was deeply pessimistic about the future. What would happen when their supplies ran out? What would happen when the summer ended? What would happen if and when the enemy came? Most of all, she fretted about being completely out of contact with her beloved son, not knowing what was happening to him or where he was. One morning, she said she had woken in the night to find Dieter standing at the foot of her bed. The vision – for that is what it was – stayed with her for the rest of her life. She did not tell anyone that day what she thought it meant, but years after would say: "It was at that point that I knew Dieter was dead."

Outwardly, Minna suppressed her unhappiness and anxiety by keeping busy. She took over as quartermistress of the lodge and ran the kitchen for all four families. Eki said: "As provisions, we had simply rice, flour and a few tins of pork: for the main meal there was either rice with pork or pork with rice."

The adults fretted, but for the children, this was a wonderland. None of them, confined in Berlin for the last seven years, could remember seeing mountains before, let alone playing in them. Eki recalled: "For Rudi and me, the whole thing was somehow like an adventure; we had no idea at all about the reasons, background or realities. We played outside mostly and strolled through the countryside. The winter was nearly at an end and already it smelled of spring. The steep mountain meadows were more like marshlands; in spite of wet feet we found it marvellous."

It was not so marvellous when one of Eki's milk teeth became infected. There were no doctors or dentists at hand in the mountains. Someone found a pair of pliers.

Anne took the boys down to the lake and taught Rudi how to swim. "How do I do it?" the boy asked, his teeth chattering, for the water was icy cold. "Like this," she said, demonstrating with a front-crawl motion of her arms. Rudi leapt in and thrashed around in a makeshift doggy paddle. He had the safeguard of having his big sister with him. There was just one problem: Anne had never learned to swim herself.

While the children played outside, there must have been a growing sense of panic and despair among the adults in the hut. What could they do? Food was running short and their contact with the outside world – a radio in the hut – was giving them nothing but bad news. On 30th April, the day Karl marked his 52nd birthday, Hitler shot himself. The month of May began with a news bulletin on the radio from Berlin: "It is reported from the Führer's headquarters that our Führer, Adolf Hitler, has fallen this afternoon at his command post in the Reich Chancellery, fighting to the last breath against Bolshevism and for Germany." The people huddled round the radio must have known from the tone and content of the subsequent bulletins that defeat was imminent.

As their stay in the mountains went on into May, the snow melted still farther from the meadows and, with more access to their surroundings, the children grew more adventurous. Rudi was the eldest and the leader of the gang. One day, he took his child platoon up and over a ridge and down into the next valley. Rudi remembered spying a scattering of debris: "By that time, the German forces had moved out, or had been driven out. We found an abandoned *Kübelwagen* [a German jeep] and got inside."

"There was a dead soldier in the back with a bullet through his head," said Eki.

"No," said Rudi, "if there had been someone in the back, I would have remembered that."

"I sat in the driver's seat and tried out all sorts of things," Rudi went on. "Then I turned the starter and found the engine going round and round. Vroom, room, room. That was smashing. We pretended we were moving along, and then suddenly I looked up and saw a British* helmet in the woods. I dived out of the jeep and the rest all followed me all the way back up to the hut. I was running and shouting: 'The English are here, the English are here!' We were all frightened because of what might happen to us. They were enemies after all, and we were all bad."

Towards the end of that first week of May, a handful of tired and dishevelled Wehrmacht soldiers who had fled from the advancing US army turned up at the hut. An American soldier described the type: "the muddy, weary GI Joe of the German army with a week's growth of beard, a long and ill-fitting grey-green overcoat that was muddy from lying on the wet ground behind an MG 42 [a machine gun] and a duckbill-cap". The soldiers demanded the rest of the families' food. Minna and Karl refused, insisting that they must save what little they had left for their own children.

The rebuffed soldiers gained revenge of a sort. They shambled down the valley, encountering other soldiers spilling out of the woods, throwing their weapons into bushes, ditches and even – when they reached Schliersee – a swimming pool. In the town, the Americans had set up a base. The Wehrmacht soldiers gave themselves up, ingratiating themselves with their captors by telling them exactly where a bunch of Nazis were hiding up in the mountains.

Listening to the hut radio on 8th May, the SS officers took in the news that the German army had surrendered. They took off their uniforms and buried them outside under some trees, returning to the hut in civilian clothing. On that same day, or possibly the day after, a US jeep containing four heavily armed soldiers drove up the track towards the hut. The jeep halted a little way short of the dwelling and the men continued stealthily on foot. The first

---

* Misidentified or misremembered – the soldier Rudi saw would have been American.

person they encountered was Anne. One of the soldiers ordered her to turn round, then thrust his gun between her shoulder blades and demanded that she lead them to the SS officers. The terrified young woman took the armed soldiers to the hut, and walked from door to door, pleading with the men inside to give themselves up.

For the one and only time in their accounts of the war years, the versions related by Rudi and Eki of what happened next differ significantly. Eki told the story that was given to him years later of a disdainful and farcical act of humiliation carried out by the American soldiers. The four fathers, lined up in the open, were told to dig up their uniforms, then put them on and come down the mountain the next day to report to US army headquarters and hand themselves in.

Rudi's take on the surrender of his father and the other three men is more visceral and is so precise, so vivid, that it is hard to believe he did not see it with his own eyes. He told how the men, standing in their uniforms with their hands tied behind their backs, were made to climb into the front of a broken-down *Kübelwagen*. Karl was ordered to sit next to the driver. Behind him, a soldier held a rifle to the back of his neck. A US jeep towed the *Kübelwagen*, and each time the vehicle stopped or hit a rut, Karl's forehead slammed against the dashboard. Every time the vehicle lurched, the back of his head bashed into the muzzle of the rifle.

It is possible that both stories are correct. Perhaps Rudi went with his father, or followed him with the rest of the families down the mountainside, then witnessed the surrender take place in the town itself. Whatever the exact detail, it was an act that still made him conclude, 65 years later: "And then they took him away. The bastards!"

20

Fighting came very late to the lakeside resort of Schliersee. The advancing American army did not reach the town until the very last week of the war. Not that Schliersee had been without its share of suffering already. Most of the young men had gone to war: many did not come back. The tiny church graveyard bears witness in its memorial stones. The Greger family lost their sons Michael, Ferdinand and Fridolin in January, February and April of 1944. Both men of the Mühlberger household, father and son, were killed.

Fifteen-year-old Peppi Eckmaier was too young to go to the front, but said that like all the boys of the town, he had wanted to belong to the Hitler Youth. Most of all, he said, they wanted to don the uniform and wear the trappings of the regime, though he emphasised that it was without any thought of doing anyone any harm.

The US army reached the outskirts of Schliersee on 4th May. What was left of the German army had already made for the mountains, so the Americans entered the town almost unopposed – some townspeople claimed they shot a mother and son as they came through the streets, mistaking them for soldiers. However, two Hitler Youth teenagers refused to surrender, and holed up in a large house from morning until evening. For some reason, the US forces did not storm the house – perhaps the boys had taken hostages. On the following morning, some captured German soldiers persuaded the teenagers to give themselves up. Peppi Eckmaier recalled: "The Americans made them stand against the wall of the *Rathaus* [the town hall]. They were there at 3 o' clock. I watched to see what would happen next – we all did. At 6 o' clock we all had to go inside.* Nobody ever saw or heard anything of them ever again."

Within a week, the Americans had combed the mountains, rounding up the beaten, demoralised German soldiers and bringing them down to the lake to march in rows three abreast. Ten thousand men of the Wehrmacht were taken through the town and encamped on the big meadows of Breitenbach on the north-west shore of the lake. The Americans slung up barbed-wire enclosures around them. The men slept out in the open, and spring nights in the Alps are often cold. Some locals claimed the soldiers were not fed in this makeshift prisoner-of-war camp, but they would stay there for several weeks, so they must have been given something, even if it was not a great deal.

The occupying army was deeply suspicious of the townspeople, believing that the area was harbouring a nest of Nazis… and so it proved. On the south side of town, at Neuhaus, they found Hans Frank, the brutal former governor-general of Poland, who had fled Krakow and brought some souvenirs with him – paintings by Rembrandt, Rubens and Leonardo da Vinci. When he was arrested, Frank tried to cut his own throat, and later tried to slit his wrists. The hangman's noose at Nuremberg would do the job properly a year later. Joachim Peiper was caught too – a former adjutant to Himmler, whose name was associated with a string of war crimes,

---

* The US army imposed a nightly 6pm curfew on the town.

including the massacre of captured US soldiers at Malmedy. And of course, word spread through the town about the gang of SS men who had hidden up in the *Schwarzenkopfhütte*. Peppi Eckmaier remembered the excitement as the townspeople waited to see them brought down from the mountains.

Once their husbands and fathers had been taken away, there was nothing the families in their Alpine cabin could do but fall on the mercy of their conquerors. They had precious little food left, nothing to do and nowhere to go. They gathered up all the belongings they could carry and made their way on foot down to Schliersee.

The US army had requisitioned a shabby, bug-ridden hotel in front of the railway station, called the Alpenrose, and there they housed the families of Nazis who had been taken away. The Niemanns were among the last to take up residence and so, instead of having the choice of front-facing rooms with a view over the lake, they were left with only a single room at the back, a poky cell with a small window. Cramped though it was for four people, it proved a small blessing. The hotel had supposedly been disinfected before all the families moved into it, but only the rooms at the rear had actually been treated. Late every night, the Niemanns could hear the cries of children at the front of the hotel as the bedbugs began to bite.

These were hard times for Minna and her children. The hotel was stigmatised by local people, who nicknamed it the *Nazischwein-haus* (Nazi pigsty) and jeered and mocked its occupants. Bavarians under American command rationed the occupants to a single slice of bread each per day, saying: "This is how you Nazi swine can live here." Anne noticed how hungry her little brothers were. One day, the bread rations came round and she said: "Give the boys my slice of bread. I'll smoke a cigarette."

The family soon discovered that American soldiers had food – lots of it, and began bartering with the enemy. Their chief negotiator was seven-year-old Eki, who gazed innocently and helplessly into soldiers' eyes and drove a soft bargain. Minna saw all their valuables traded – binoculars and camera equipment sold fast and not especially profitably. Anne felt the camera itself was too valuable to leave to her little brother and went off to do business herself. The soldier who bought it said he didn't have enough money on him, but he would come back the next day. He never did.

Anne grumbled to others about the American army's deceitful behaviour. Others said the Americans were thieves; they stole food from the farms, they even stole women's jewellery. And in Anne's eyes, they had stolen her father. Worse was yet to come.

The Niemann family resorted to desperate measures for food. An ailing mule (it was bound to die soon) turned up in the street. Minna persuaded a butcher to despatch it and cut it up for them. They ate roast mule in various ways for the next few days, though how they managed to cook it, nobody remembered.

At least some of the townspeople were in a similar situation. Peppi Eckmaier's mother went out foraging in the meadows and picked a plant he remembered she called "white spinach" to supplement their meagre diet.

In time, the children went out to play, as children the world over do. And kind American soldiers played with the children, as soldiers always have done in war zones when peace returns. They made little paper berets for the Nazi kids. One soldier gave Rudi a loan of his US army helmet, a fellow GI photographed the boy wearing it (but presumably not using the Niemanns' stolen camera) and would later give him a print of the picture. Rudi's gang now played soldiers, running around in American headgear: it must have been the most bizarre scene for an onlooker. Who did the children imagine they were fighting and which side were they pretending to be fighting for?

The children's main playground was a junkyard in front of the railway tracks to the side of the hotel. Here they scrambled over and toyed with all sorts of military debris. By now they were mixing with Bavarian children. Their new companions may have talked with strange accents, but they were children and playmates just the same. The big attraction for the junkyard explorers was a broken-down Panzer armoured reconnaissance vehicle, an eight-wheeled beast complete with a turret that was the next best thing to a tank. Eventually, one of the boys managed to clamber inside. He must have put a foot or hand wrong, for seconds later the vehicle was rocked by a huge explosion. The boy was badly injured; he may well have died.

The fervent Nazi mother of Heike, Anke and Elke gave birth to a baby son while they were staying in the hotel. She did not call the child Wibke, as Minna had predicted. She named the boy Eckhart.

Minna was well aware that the family could not stay in Schliersee. Here they were in limbo. Supposing that Karl and Dieter were still alive, there would have been no way for them to contact the rest of their family. Minna decided that they should make for Hameln and go to her mother's house once again. But heading 400 miles to the north would be no easy task. At the end of May 1945, Germany was a country thronged with refugees; there were something like eight million people criss-crossing the nation in search of some-where to go. And years of Allied bombing had obliterated roads and railway tracks everywhere.

Schliersee had a railway station but no ticket office. The nearest source of tickets was Miesbach, about five miles away, and word of mouth had it that there was a train that would go north as far as Munich, although nobody knew when it would arrive in Schliersee or when it would leave. The famous reputation for German punctuality had been blown to pieces. Eki described the train time-tables as being like something written by the Grimm brothers – full of complete fantasy. Nevertheless, it was their only realistic hope and Anne volunteered to be ticket collector. On 5th June, she was registered as a citizen of Schliersee (residing in the Hotel Alpenrose) and with this proof of her identity and abode, she was equipped to purchase tickets to travel to a defined destination.

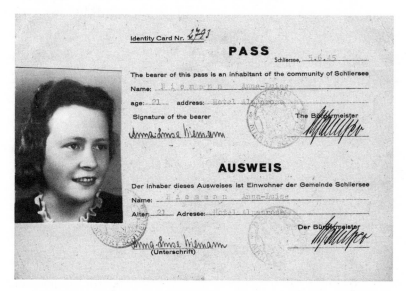

Day after day, Anne set off and completed a ten-mile round trip to Miesbach without success. Her treks through the country-side were highly dangerous in those chaotic weeks and the pretty 21-year-old walking all alone was at grave risk.

Eventually, Anne managed to buy rail tickets for them all. The boys were overjoyed at the prospect of beginning the next stage of their great adventure. Emboldened by the knowledge that they were leaving, they hung out of their window and taunted their erstwhile playmates in the street below, shouting: *"Bierbayern! Bierbayern!"* (beery Bavarians). The Schliersee kids responded in kind with *"Saupreussen!"* (Prussian pigs). The truce was over and both sides gave vent to longstanding north-south prejudices. However, the little Prussian pigs were premature with their insults: the train was delayed by a day and so the Niemann boys stayed in their room, too afraid of reprisals to even go out into the street.

On a mid-June morning, the family crossed the road to the railway station and stood on a platform packed with people wanting to leave the Alps. The doors of the one train of the week opened and there was a scramble to get on board. Eki recalled: "Mutti, Anne and Rudi were on the train and I was still standing on the platform with a gigantic rucksack on my back. The train was already in motion! Fortunately a foreign traveller grasped the situation and lifted me, rucksack and all, through the open window, where my family happily took delivery of me."

21

On the day of Karl's arrest, the US jeep towed the broken-down, open-topped German jeep, full of SS officers, slowly through the town. People stood and watched the victors pulling along the chariot of the vanquished. In all likelihood, the American soldiers were tense and nervous, transporting men they thought could be important and potentially dangerous war criminals. As they were passing the house of an elderly man who was pottering in his garden, one of the soldiers aimed his pistol and shot the man dead. It could have been an act of wanton brutality. Karl always saw it that way. But perhaps the old man raised a spade, a glint of metal that could have been a gun…

Karl and his fellow officers were offloaded into the lakeside meadows where 10,000 soldiers of the Wehrmacht were already caged behind a makeshift fence of barbed wire. The US army treated the soldiers as Disarmed Enemy Forces, which meant they did not receive the standard of treatment they would have under the Geneva Convention as prisoners of war. One Schliersee resident claimed the men were given no food. Whatever the truth of that allegation, they would have certainly received harsh treatment from their captors, who lacked the resources and manpower to treat them much better.

And the men of the SS, accustomed to the methods of the Gestapo and easily identifiable by their uniforms, would have half expected to be taken out and shot at any moment.

Karl spent a number of days and nights out in the open, behind barbed wire as he had been 25 years before. And with plenty of time to while away, he looked out over the lake and became familiar with features of the town on the other side. He could make out the railway station not far from the shore. And his eyes must have rested on the four-storey building behind it, the Hotel Alpenrose...

Had they occupied rooms at the front of the hotel, and had they still been in possession of their bartered binoculars, the family might have seen Karl every day. As it was, they remained on opposite shores of the lake, in complete ignorance of each other.

The children had not heard anything of Karl for more than a month when they boarded the train for Munich, the first leg of their long journey. It was dreadfully overcrowded, crammed with the displaced and dispossessed. Rudi recalled that every train was like that as, over the next few weeks, they made their way north, sometimes sleeping in stations, sometimes in schools, waiting for the next connection. There might be a room with beds, or they might have to sleep on benches, or on the floor. One night the children slept on school desks.

Somewhere on the journey, they may have spent the night in a tent. Just weeks before she died, Anne confided to her granddaughter Stephanie that "a friend" was raped by an American soldier at that time and that she could hear her screams from the tent next door. She told a similar story to her other granddaughter, Kirsten. Eki said that Anne had no friends on that journey. The full story of what happened that spring died with her.

Ninety miles short of their destination, the family was taken to a so-called displaced persons camp outside Kassel run by the

British Army. A refugee camp in all but name, the place was full
of lost souls – many had abandoned their homes to flee west from
the Russians, others were wanting to go north, south or east. It
was a disease-ridden camp crowded with confusion, despair and
malnourished people. Eki recalled that Anne had caught crab lice
and was itching with discomfort. But worst of all, they met a
wounded German soldier there. He told them he had been fighting
near Nuremberg and that he had been the last commander of
Dieter's unit. He said that the unit had been surrounded by American troops and the men annihilated. "I am the only survivor," he
told them. Devastating though the news was, Eki remembered his
mother holding out a glimmer of hope. Dieter had at least been
fighting on the Western Front rather than against the Russians,
she said. He might only have been wounded. He might still be
alive.

At last, the family reached Hameln. Loaded with baggage for the
last time on their epic journey – or so they thought – they walked
from the station to Adolfstrasse, and stood on the doorstep of the
house Minna's father had built. She rang the bell. There was no
answer. She knocked on the door. After a while, the door opened
a little and there was Minna's mother peering through the crack.
Minna explained the family's predicament and asked to be let in.
The old lady looked at her for a moment, then said: "Could you
not go to your brother Karl's?"* Minna's sister-in-law Mimi came to
the door and it swung open a little more. Was this the welcoming
counter-order? "Can't you go somewhere else?" she asked. Minna
said nothing in reply. Her mother shut the door, leaving Minna
and her children still standing on the step.

---

* Lina Schwenker was by that time suffering from dementia. She had no son
called Karl.

Once again, the Niemanns had no option but to go to the authorities for help. And the authorities, the soldiers and administrators of the British army of occupation, were struggling to house 50,000 refugees in a town of 50,000 inhabitants. They were less than sympathetic towards the unhelpful sitting residents in Adolfstrasse 2: "You have the rooms – you take your family in," they decreed. The family squeezed inside. Anne, Rudi and Eki shared the attic room in Onkel Willi and Aunt Mimi's flat, while Minna suffered the indignity of having to share a bedroom with her now demented mother who had so often neglected her.

Karl had disappeared altogether from their lives. Minna heard nothing at all of him all that year. Was he dead or alive? What could she say to her young sons? Why had their father been taken away? She took practical steps and began to draw on Karl's savings, using money from the accounts he had set up for the children to sustain the family. It would not be enough on its own. Anne went out to look for a job. A building opposite the Münsterkirche had been turned into the Pipers' Club, a meeting and eating place run by Germans for British soldiers. Pretty Anne was hired as a waitress, together with a number of other young German women, chosen for their looks.

The soldiers gave the waitresses cigarettes as tips, but heavy smoker Anne refrained from lighting up. Every night, after hours – and they were long hours – the women would gather up the soldiers' leftovers and share them out. Then they would each take their portion of food back to their needy families. They were the lucky ones – in the autumn of 1945, the average German subsisted on 1,200 calories per day, less than half the quantity British civilians were receiving and below the minimum an adult needs to survive in the long run.

Anne divided the Pipers' Club food equally between her own immediate family and the Schwenkers, the relations who had turned them away at the door not so long before. She gave the cigarettes to her mother, who would take them to a little outbuilding in the courtyard of Adolfstrasse 2. The hut was the workplace of cobbler Johann Kasczmarek. He had a steady stream of customers but not many were on errands connected with boots or shoes. The cobbler's workshop operated as Hameln's black market central and a stack of cigarettes could be exchanged for an under-the-counter joint of pork or a leg of lamb. Johann's illicit business ran through all the post-war years of hardship.

Though they were always hungry, the two boys roamed widely and were, as ever, inveterate mischief-makers, bordering on delinquency. At school, they were nicknamed Max and Moritz, after two popular comic pranksters, one dark-haired, one fair. On the banks of the river Weser, they discovered a stash of ack-ack ammunition that had been abandoned by the German army. Back to Adolfstrasse they went, to collect the biggest of Onkel Willi's four-wheeled trollies from the courtyard. Who took notice of two little boys pulling a loaded trolley through the streets of Hameln? Once they had taken their explosive find back to base, Rudi prised open the cartridges with pliers and drilled out the gunpowder. He refilled one of the cartridges to the top with gunpowder, put his home-made bomb on the window ledge of Johann's workshop and set a fuse.

"Boom!" said Rudi. "Ooh, what a stink there was in the neighbourhood. And it made a mess! But it didn't break the windows somehow and Johannn wasn't amused."

One Sunday, while the congregation prayed in the Münsterkirche, Rudi and Eki crept outside and let themselves into the crypt through a skylight. Rudi pushed back the stone lid of a coffin and took out a skull. He went back to Adolfstrasse and greeted his sister with: "Do you want to see my friend here?" Anne took one look at the skull under his arm and screamed.

Another skull surfaced when workmen were digging a hole close to the church. Rudi spirited it away and spent hour after hour trying to scrub it clean. Eventually, he found a place for it on the table between the two boys' beds. The now gleaming head was giving the boys a toothy grin after dark. It was too much for Eki. In the dead of night, while his brother slept, he whipped the skull away inside a blanket and dropped it down the earth closet toilet outside.

At harvest time, the boys caught mice streaming out of the fields, put them on planks of wood and pushed them out into the river to see if they could sail: "We caught one in our bedroom too and dropped it out of the window to find out if it would live."

And did it?

"No."

Rudi led a little party of juvenile miscreants one night. They shinned up the gaslights, one by one, and turned them off. The whole neighbourhood was in darkness.

With each passing month, any lingering hopes that Dieter had somehow survived shrank. And Christmas passed without news of Karl. In January 1946, the family finally received a letter that brought great joy. Karl was alive and interned at Moosburg, a former prisoner-of-war camp in Bavaria within the American zone of occupation.

What would become of him? An international military tribunal (the so-called Nuremberg Trials) had begun in November. The Nazi leaders were on trial for their lives, but the prosecution was also setting out a case for criminalising membership of the SS. The family must have been aware of the strong likelihood that Karl himself would stand trial. In the meantime, all through 1946, they waited and exchanged infrequent letters with their imprisoned father and husband.

That year brought near starvation to towns and cities throughout

Germany, including Hameln itself. The US administration had resisted giving assistance. The initial view of Governor-General Clay – "I feel that the Germans should suffer from hunger and from cold as I believe such suffering is necessary to make them realise the consequences of a war which they caused" – was widely backed until it was calculated that between two and three million civilians might die. In Congress, Senator William Langer advocated relief: "Among the crimes with which this [German] leadership has been charged is the crime of systematic and mass starvation of racial or political minorities or opponents.... Yet to our utter horror, we discover that our own policies have merely spread those same conditions."

Those policies of starvation were reversed. Rudi remembered being a beneficiary of US aid at school. Each pupil was given bags of peanuts and there was a soup kitchen: "There was soup with loads of sausages floating about at the top. The older pupils helped themselves to the sausages so by the time we came there were none left." The enterprising boy roamed widely to find extra food for the family. In April, he took to fields flooded by the Weser to catch eels for the pot, although they were no treat for him. "I hated them," he said.

Rudi was soon to receive untold delights – cakes and chewing gum from a friend of their sister. A special friend whose arrival would alter the course of his life.

22

Most of Karl's colleagues were caught… eventually. The war was coming to an end when his immediate boss Josef Opperbeck and his SS party halted in the Alpine village of Sachrang, just fifteen miles east of Spitzingsee. They took to the countryside, where they buried several cases filled with documents. Then they stood up, shook hands and promised on their honour that what they had done would remain a secret between them. However, when the US army occupied the village and the men gave themselves up, one of their number, a man whom Opperbeck later referred to as "a collaborator", went in a car with an American escort party to the hiding place and the cases were dug up. Opperbeck was taken to Dachau, to begin his internment in the former concentration camp.

It was a long time before Karl Bestle was run to ground. He and his wife had fled Berlin in the company of a carpenter to the town of Schwarzenbek, near Hamburg, and Bestle and his accomplice set themselves up in a carpentry business. It was not until February 1946 that he was found out. The runaway officer was detained in what had been Neuengamme concentration camp until August 1947, when he was shipped south. Bestle was sent to Dachau, this time as a captive and not a captor.

Oswald Pohl had been masquerading under the name of Ludwig Gniss as a farm hand in northern Germany, when he was discovered and arrested in May 1946. He had scratches on his face which he said had been inflicted by his British captors: "I don't hold it against the men who beat me because undoubtedly there are ruffians of every nationality and the English are not exceptions."

Karl's camp at Moosburg, west of Munich, had been known as Stalag VII/A only a few weeks before, and the security trappings of a prisoner-of-war camp remained – double barbed-wire fences around the perimeter, with coils of barbed wire between the fences, and watchtowers located at regular intervals. The key difference now was the changing of the guard that had taken place, with the soldiers of the Wehrmacht being replaced with American troops.

Many of the soldiers posted as guards had shared the experiences of Rifleman Donald Wilson, who had taken part in the liberation of Mauthausen concentration camp and was, in the words of his son, "a tough guy". Like Wilson, these soldiers had seen evidence of extreme brutality, and, understandably, wanted a measure of revenge, to mete out some of the punishment that had been given to concentration camp inmates to those identified and imprisoned as perpetrators.

Karl was initiated into the camp by being funnelled into a hut with a corrugated roof, where a line of US soldiers tore his insignia – his Iron Cross, lapel pips and Cross of Honour – from his uniform. He stepped into the shack as SS-Hauptsturmführer Niemann and walked out as prisoner number 209023, Civilian Internment Camp No. 6 of the US Third Army. He was given a fork, a spoon and a towel that was about the size of a large handkerchief.

Two-thirds of the 12,000 internees were political functionaries of the regime – card-carrying party members who had served in the military, or as mayors, treasurers or in some other official capacity.

There were 400 women – some of whom had been concentration camp guards. Karl was one of a group of SS officers sent to block 8, a line of eight wooden barracks next to a penal barrack hut. One of the lower functionaries commented that "these higher officials gave our camp a certain character".

During the war, Karl's barrack hut had been equipped with bunk beds – quite possibly built under Karl's own overall supervision. But there was no furniture left now – everything had been stripped out when the Allies left; windows were broken, and there were holes in the roof. For the next six months, until rough bunk beds were installed, Karl slept on the floor of his hut. One inmate made himself a makeshift pillow out of grass. It was soon taken away.

The departing soldiers had left tiny mementoes of their stay: the huts were riddled with lice and fleas. Karl had been sprayed with white DDT powder when he arrived in Moosburg. It kept the bugs off… for a while.

Food – or lack of it – soon became a serious issue. A Protestant minister among the internees called Klaus von Eickstedt noted that:

Morning breakfast put us in great consternation, because we were told that the thick slice of bread would be enough for the whole day. Lunch… was watery soup… with peas that put together barely filled a tablespoon… After the first few weeks some comrades no longer had the strength to present themselves at the daily roll-call, others fell down in a faint at this, not to mention those who were beginning to fill the hospital. Was it any wonder that some comrades sought to commit suicide under these conditions or lost their lives while trying to escape from the camp? We thought that this criminal treatment would be short-lived. But this was not so.

Inmate Paul Schmidt concurred: "We seriously thought the Americans intended us to perish."

A number of accounts point to other forms of mistreatment. Some prisoners said they were subjected to regular beatings. And there were random acts of violence. Georg Miller wrote:

In the autumn of 1945, I was about 10 metres from the security fence with Stanislaus Schmid. As Schmid bent down to a dandelion, he was shot by a guard through the carotid artery... One night that autumn, one of the inmates put up a wooden plaque with the names of 20 inmates murdered so far in this or similar ways written with chalk. The panel was removed the next day by the camp administration.

The prisoners were told they were to have no contact with the outside world. One claimed that an announcement was made that any such attempt would be punished with death. Camp minister Klaus von Eickstedt commented:

No one knew whether their loved ones were still alive. This uncertainty wore down the mental resilience of the prisoners even more than the physical hunger. Many were now stuck in a state of dull despair or personal anxiety as to whether they would even get through this existence. How quickly outward appearance and "white European civility" disappeared then when the basest instincts were awakened by hunger and the last vestiges of human dignity were eliminated. It was painful to watch again and again how comrades, who one knew had had respectable positions in their bourgeois existence, were carried away... as wild animals they pounced on cigarette butts that had been thrown away by the American soldiers, then went on to smoke them.

The military governor of Bavaria paid a visit at the end of August. General George Patton was a hero of the war and an embarrassment of the peace. His outspoken comments were laced with anti-Semitism and drenched with a hatred of Communism. Worst of all, in pressing for Germany to act as a buffer against Russia, he openly supported exoneration of Nazi war criminals. They were, he said, "just like Democrats or Republicans".

Patton was already predisposed to be favourable towards the inmates when he went into Moosburg. He stood before them and declared that their internment was "sheer madness". When he saw the state of the prisoners in the barracks and the camp hospital filled with inmates afflicted with typhus and food deficiency-related diseases, he ordered instant action. Rations went up from 900 to 4,000 calories a day, well above what civilians outside were receiving. They fell soon afterwards, but never again to starvation levels.

Karl and his fellow inmates were finally allowed to write home just before Christmas, to say they were still alive. A single postcard a month was permitted in the first year of confinement. From 1946, families were allowed to send food and some items of clothing.

Before long, inmates had radio contact with the outside world, enabling them to grasp something of what was going on beyond the wire. They knew of the Stuttgart Declaration of October 1945, in which a council of Protestant ministers called on all Germans to address their personal responsibilities for their actions during the war: "By us infinite wrong was committed against many peoples and countries," it stated. The idea of collective guilt was welcomed by minister von Eickstedt, who saw that it carried support from the "reasonable and considerate elements in the camp... as noble and decent".

But among others, he paints a picture of outright denial:

It was quite impossible to talk to non-Christians of guilt, of the personal guilt of the individual, let alone that of a group, a party, the government or even the German people. Comrades in the camp, no doubt partly responsible for what had happened in Germany during the last years due to their previous position in the party... considered themselves as victims of a leadership which, originally motivated by pure will, had been weakened and crushed by sabotage, betrayal, infidelity, and occasionally the inability of individuals... The reasons for such an attitude were deep, for the most part often unconscious attempts at self-justification and self-assertion.

The prisoners' hatred was directed at one of the main architects of the Stuttgart Declaration in particular. Pastor Martin Niemöller, a former U-boat commander of the Great War and a Nazi in the early years, openly agonised over his own guilt and urged others to do likewise. When von Eickstedt gave a talk on Niemöller in camp, the advertising poster was defaced.

In the two years that Karl spent in Moosburg, there was punishment aplenty and it seemed to foster solidarity among many inmates, a hardening of beliefs – the exact opposite of what would have been intended by their captors. There were no serious efforts by the American authorities at rehabilitation of the prisoners. There were only crude attempts to make the inmates address what they had done – in March 1946, for example, they were instructed to write affidavits explaining the extent of their involvement in the *Kristallnacht* attack on the Jews in 1938. It was no surprise that a Nazi organisation which called itself the Union of Former Ortsgruppenleiter* began within the camp.

Legal judgment began with the show trials of Hitler's henchmen

---

* Nazi Party local group leaders.

in Nuremberg. The so-called "golden pheasants", the medalled, preening leaders such as Göring, who had bolted from Berlin at the end of the war, went before the court for the first time in November 1945. The case dragged on. Inmates listening to reports on the radio grumbled at their own inability to influence the proceedings. One wrote that though there were thousands of SS members and political leaders in Moosburg, none had been given a chance to give evidence: "A good lesson for the unteachable!" he declared, with a bucketful of irony. "The mayor of the camp, an intern, has sent a protest to Nuremberg! But whether it will arrive?..."

By early 1947, more than half of the 12,000 Moosburg inmates had been freed. Those like Karl, who still awaited their turn, were agitating for something to happen. Among his denazification papers, Karl had submitted an article that set out the grievances of those men. Only the first page survives:

Forgotten behind barbed wire?

On the situation of the people who are internees in the Moosburg detention camp (Upper Bavaria) in the British* zone.

1.) Still today, two years after the capitulation, around 640 Germans whose home is in the British zone are detained in the camp in Moosburg. 40 of them are from Hamburg, 240 from Niedersachsen, 270 from Nordrhein-Westfalen, 80 from Schleswig Holstein, and eight from Lippe. Numerous Germans are also still detained in camps in the American zone. The fate of the internees is unknown. There is no tangible prospect for them that their cases will be examined and that they will ultimately be released to return to their homes.

---

* A significant factual error which suggests that this polemic was not written by Karl or any of the other internees. Moosburg was in the American rather than the British zone of occupation.

2.) Under American administration of the Moosburg camp, the internees from the British zone had already requested that they be sent home for their denazification. The request has been without success. When in Oct. 1946, the Bavarian administration took over control of the Moosburg camp, the internees were promised by the former Ministry of State for Special Affairs that (by a soon to be implemented rule about zone exchange) they would be transferred to their home cities. Subsequently, further assurances were made in addition to this promise. Yet, none of all of this materialised. Instead, the internees are told today that there is no prospect of them being repatriated in the near future. They are left without any idea of what will happen to them, in particular when and how the denazification will take place. Hence, for the internees, the eventual return to their homes is in the unforeseeable distant future.

3.) The here-mentioned circumstances are apt to make the already difficult situation of the internees in the British zone even more unbearable. They will lead to serious psychological distress and unpredictable consequences. The already difficult position of the internees is due to the following:

a) The majority of internees in the British zone were, before their automatic arrest, soldiers of the Wehrmacht and were separated from their families for over seven years.

b) Since about half a year ago, the cases of those detained in the US zone have been dealt with by the denazification courts (at the camps), while the cases of those soldiers detained at camps in the British zone remain unresolved. At the same time, the internees have seen that denazification is taking place in their home areas... while they are just left waiting in the camps.

c) After being completely cut off from their families and loved ones from early summer 1945 to early 1946, the internees who are based

in the British zone have only under greatest hardships the – [the
article was cut off here at the end of the page]

It must have been important during this period for inmates to have had documentation to show their true identity. It may have expedited legal proceedings. There were certainly plenty of Nazis masquerading under false names. Karl found a scrap of paper and rounded up half a dozen fellow inmates to provide written testimony:

Moosburg, 5.3.47
Statutory declaration

We, the signatories of this, herewith declare that Mr Karl Niemann
born 30.4.93 in Hemeringen, former SS-Hauptsturmführer *of the*
economic management administration office Berlin was promoted to
this rank on 20 April 1940. After this time and until the collapse of
the regime, he was promoted no more.

Early in the spring of 1947, Karl left Moosburg, but he was moved, not released. His second place of internment was destined to be in his own state of Lower Saxony. It was just one hundred miles and a full year away from his family.

23

"The area around the camp is anything but idyllic. The country is exceptionally poor... with areas overgrown with heather, marshes, the reed, interrupted here and there by some fir trees and wind-bent, stunted birches... Nine out of twelve months it rains, or the sky is shrouded in fog. For the remainder of the year, in summer, the sun is quite warm, and the wind swirls a dust of peat and sand, which makes it almost impossible to breathe. You think you are in the Sahara." – Gaston Aufrere, Allied POW at Sandbostel

On his first day as civilian governor of Sandbostel Civil Internment Camp No. 2, Lieutenant-Colonel (retired) Edward Roger Vickers addressed his charges. Nearly all of them had been members of the SS, either as officials or as concentration camp guards. The British ex-officer began: "Gentlemen! During the Great War, I was in a German prisoner-of-war camp. I was treated as a gentleman. I would like to treat you in just the same way." An inmate declared: "Incredulous and doubtful, we heard the speech of the new governor that suggested much would change for the better in the coming year. Somehow it felt as if the words brought a great release. But most of all – you felt you were spoken to for the first time as a human being. And that worked wonders!"

The new governor had not only been a POW, he had also previously run a camp full of them. Leuitenant-Colonel Vickers had supervised captured German soldiers at Featherstone, Yorkshire, in the last years of the Second World War. His role had been to rule, but also, from 1944 onwards, to rehabilitate his prisoners for a life in their homeland after Hitler.

One of his first acts at Sandbostel was to order the barbed-wire fences and watchtowers of the former POW camp to be pulled down. Vickers set up a camp council, so that the inmates would effectively self-govern daily life in the camp. He instructed the council to create a camp constitution. Decisions were made through universal voting in secret ballots.

The men were encouraged to produce a camp newspaper, which they named *Der Windstoss* (*The Gust of Wind*) after the ever-present "breeze". One of them interviewed the British camp intelligence officer, who gave an insight into a political system that most of them had never known or could barely remember: "One of the most important principles of democracy is freedom of speech," declared the officer. As a practical example, he promised "that if anyone expresses his opinion in open discussion or in the camp newspaper there will be no adverse consequences". This must have been scarcely believable for men who had lived through fifteen years of totalitarianism.

Vickers set up training courses, preparing inmates for professional life after captivity. He encouraged cultural life too – concerts, theatre productions and talks became the norm. Many internees played sports.

By the time Karl arrived at Sandbostel, it was more like an open prison. For the next year, he would be in an environment that would act as a stepping stone to civilian life in a democratic society. Whereas there had been, at Moosburg, very little work to stave off boredom, here there was wholesale occupation in meaningful employment. The men were sent off daily to work as far as twelve miles away. There were no guards sent with them: the prisoners were asked to sign a form promising on their word of honour that they would return.

For all the humane treatment that Karl received, one thing would have always been uppermost in his mind during this time. He had to face trial and punishment. He was already being punished, for by the time he entered Sandbostel, he had served two years of internment. And whether he knew it or not, he had already made an appearance of sorts in court.

The protracted show trial of Hitler's associates at Nuremberg had concluded in October 1946. Immediately afterwards, the US broke through fracturing relationships between the Allies to launch, independently, a series of twelve trials against lesser war criminals, under the jurisdiction of American military courts. The fourth of these trials focussed on the leaders of the SS administrative organisation, the WVHA. Its official title was The United States of America vs Oswald Pohl et al.

Karl was just one level of management away from being called in person. His immediate superior, Josef Opperbeck, was summoned from internment in Dachau and spent three nights in all in Nuremberg prison, facing interrogators by day. Karl's own appearance in the courtroom in Nuremberg was limited to box 555. The prosecution offered two papers written by Karl as part of their evidence, including his 55-page statement of accounts for SS industries for 1943 (pages 117–22). They threw 850 documents into the ring; the defence team batted back more than a thousand.

In the dock were Pohl and seventeen of his most senior managers. They were chosen not so much as individuals, but as representatives of the different departments of the WVHA. They even sat in the dock according to the areas for which they had responsibility: the SS business managers together, the concentration camp administrators grouped a little farther down the row of seats, for example. When all the lies, denials of responsibility, claims of ignorance and self-justifications had been extracted over a full year, Karl's bosses learned their fate. Oswald Pohl was sentenced to death by hanging, as were three others. Eleven were given long prison sentences, three were acquitted.

A process had long since been set in train to bring Karl himself to justice. Even before the war had ended, a group of German exiles in America had worked on methods for cleansing Europe of National Socialism. They called it denazification. According to a generally accepted definition, it meant dismantling the Nazi Party and obliterating its influence through arresting and imprisoning its senior figures and removing party members from all government, business and cultural positions of authority.

Following the main Nuremberg trial, denazification took shape. Former Nazis objected on the grounds that it "violated an elementary legal principle... any act committed cannot be punished unless the law setting forth such punishment was in existence at the time of commission". And so, careful not to offend wider German sensibilities, the trials became tribunals and defendants were judged according to responsibilities rather than guilt. Otherwise, there were all the elements of a judicial proceeding, with a judge, prosecution, defence, the accused and – in the panel of the *Spruchgericht* (tribunal) – a jury. There was no element of compulsion to denazification – Germans only had to go to a panel if they were seeking future employment. Many senior Nazis with wealth behind them simply kept their heads down until the process was over and then slipped back into public life unchallenged.

The paper trail shows that all through Karl's confinement in

Sandbostel he was reaching out to people who might support his defence in court. In Hameln itself, Mimi Schmidt, a niece with connections, was gathering testimonies. The daughter of painter Friedrich, who had given Karl accommodation prior to the First World War, Fräulein Schmidt worked at the Hameln employment office. Linked through a network of civil service officialdom, she managed to track down three of the concentration camp inmates to whom Karl had given wartime assistance. In Vienna, she found Franz Doppler, now a university professor. In Hamburg, Karl Steiner was running a guest house. In the Austrian town of Klagenfurt, civil servant Franz Müller-Strobl came forward willingly. Other inmates may have been dead, untraceable, unwilling or unable to respond.

Hameliners able to vouch for Karl's pre-war character were hard to find – it had been almost twenty years since he had lived there. Mimi received testimony from the elderly August Meier, Karl's former manager at the Deutsche Bank, and – more tenuously – Anneliese Prael, the daughter of Karl's former landlady. Karl himself contacted his former landlord Martin Weinsteiger, still in the Dachau house where the Niemann family had lodged during the mid-1930s.

In the second half of 1947, the judicial destination for the remaining internees was determined when courts were established under German jurisdiction in the Lower Saxony town of Stade. The town prosecutors came to Sandbostel to interrogate the accused, and an office was set up in the camp to prepare the inmates for mounting their defence. Sandbostel archivist Andreas Ehresmann describes the feelings of prisoners during this period: "For the internees, a centrally important issue was the question of the likely effects of punishment on their lives after release, not only direct constraints, but also the psychological consequences of the 'stigma of criminality'."

Proceedings began with the official handover of denazification to the state of Lower Saxony in October. By the beginning of February 1948, there were 902 inmates left in Sandbostel. One month later, there were just 171. Karl was among the last of the prisoners to be released, before the camp shut down for good in April.

24

"Women are always the first to un-make the conquest and betray the conqueror – and properly, else the males' preposterous wars would continue forever, unrelieved by sanity." – Unknown WW2 American soldier/philosopher

At the end of 1945, the young women of Hameln were desperately short of love, sex and male company. Three to four million German soldiers were still in Russian prisoner-of-war camps, and millions more had been killed. At just 22 years of age, Anne feared, as those of her mother's generation had feared before, that she would never marry, and would die a lonely, childless, impoverished spinster.

Young German women had no misgivings about embracing the enemy. In an immediate post-war poll, they described British soldiers as "intelligent, self-controlled, practical, progressive, generous, peace-loving, hard-working and brave". Thousands gave their hearts or sold them for cigarettes. A jealous phrase did the rounds among German ex-soldiers and civilians: "German men have completely lost their courage. German women have completely lost their shame."

The Pipers' Club where Anne worked proved to be a dating agency, matching young British soldiers with their attractive German hostesses. Anne's fellow waitress friend Margarethe had lost her husband on the Russian front. She found love with a corporal in the Royal Signals Corps called James McLean. Anne was drawn to his best friend, another corporal, another Scot. Lanarkshire-born George Falconer was a man who – like Anne's own brother – had served in a tank regiment. He had been a Desert Rat, fighting his way through Africa and then Italy. He said he was a sportsman too – he had gone for trials before the war as a goalkeeper with top football clubs Glasgow Celtic and Wolverhampton Wanderers.

Above all, George, with his shock of coal-black hair and broad gap-toothed grin, oozed self-confidence. He had a victor's swagger. The man in the smart soldier's uniform wooed Anne with cakes and cigarettes. For a woman who had known only months of misery, here was an irresistible promise of future happiness. How much the young woman and her soldier beau with wonky teeth really got to know each other during that courtship of snatched hours between duties is questionable. George never learned German and Anne's schoolgirl English would have left her far from fluent.

George came to the Niemann home in Adolfstrasse and charmed Anne's little brothers with sweets. He introduced them to chewing gum and brought cake, lots of cake. Rudi was surprised that Anne's friend wanted to stay the night in their already crowded home. Those sleepovers had a consequence: Anne fell pregnant. George proposed to his expectant girlfriend.

Good news seemed to arrive just in time for the Anglo-German coupling. In August 1946, when Anne was three months pregnant, official word came through that British soldiers would be allowed to marry their German sweethearts, provided they had permission from their commanding officer. Though a six-month waiting period was stipulated while medical checks and paperwork were sorted out, it would be a mere formality unless there were exceptional circumstances. George duly applied for permission to marry.

The first of two obstacles fell into their path. George's unit was transferred from Hameln to a base twelve miles away. George had no transport to enable him to see his fiancée. Anne gave him a photograph of herself as a memento, writing on the back in her best English: "To my darling, so that you will think of me."

George quickly solved the immediate problem. Low in rank, high in cunning, he couldn't help noticing that military policemen hitching a lift at the side of the road had no difficulties in being picked up. Cars, jeeps and lorries stopped to offer a ride to these men of importance, easily identifiable by their distinctive white belts. George got hold of a tin of white paint. It worked a treat. George became a regular visitor to Hameln again. Minna's poor demented mother conducted her future grandson-in-law around the house, saying that it now belonged to him.

A bigger, unsurmountable blockage came. George was told his application to marry had been refused. "A blockhead of a British bureaucrat said it was unthinkable that a Scottish soldier could marry the daughter of a Nazi," said Eki. Time was running out; the soldier's term of military duty was coming to an end.

George played the stubborn card for all he was worth. Eki recalled his insistent declarations: "I will stay in Germany as long as I have to until I am allowed to marry my Annariese."* In February 1947, Anne gave birth in Adolfstrasse to a daughter, Isabelle. Faced with a corporal who was now the father of an illegitimate child, the authorities relented.

The wedding was fixed for June in Hameln's Münsterkirche, the same church where Anne's parents had married in 1921. George's fellow corporal agreed to be his best man. Who would give Anne away?

---

* A slight speech impediment caused him to swallow the letter l.

There was talk of Karl being released to go to his daughter's wedding – a word-of-honour arrangement that would allow him to attend and then return to his prison. It is possible that he was let out for a day to see the couple before they were married, but he was certainly not allowed out for the wedding itself.

Since Karl was out of the picture to give his daughter away, they asked the only man in the house, Minna's brother. Onkel Willi had been only too willing to eat the British army's cakes that Anne had brought home for the family, but he was worried about what his friends would think of him endorsing the marriage of his niece to one of the enemy. He turned the request down. The sought-after role fell to a token male, an old neighbour. Minna never forgave her brother for his betrayal.

Anne went to her wedding burdened by the shame of an illegitimate birth. She would never celebrate her big wedding anniversaries thereafter, afraid that people would do the maths and work out that her daughter had been born out of wedlock.

Nine-year-old Eki barely remembered the party after the wedding: he was drunk at the time. He had teamed up with his cousin Rolf beforehand to pick strawberries and make strawberry punch, as well as potato schnapps. Eki drank alcohol and smoked that day for the first time in his life. He was ill for a whole week afterwards.

Anne sent her absent father a photograph of her new husband. She wrote a message on the back: "My dear papa, may I present to you Mr Falconer, your son in law."

Luck ran out for George's best man and his German girlfriend shortly after the wedding. Margarethe's dead husband returned very much alive from a Russian prisoner-of-war camp. Her Scottish lover, now surplus to requirements, was posted to Palestine, where he would be shot in the head by an Israeli sniper.

The newlyweds, meanwhile, were destined for a brave new life together. Anne would travel abroad for the first time in her life to live with her husband in his home town in Scotland. Minna told Anne it was the right thing for her to do – what future was there for her in Germany?

The couple and their baby daughter took a series of trains, an overnight ferry, and still more trains, to arrive, exhausted by the journey, in the Lanarkshire mining town of Larkhall. For generations, it had the reputation of being the most sectarian town in Scotland, religious hatred supposedly triggered in the 1920s, when Irish Catholics were drafted into the mines as strikebreakers. Elsewhere in Scotland, the railings of parks and playgrounds were painted municipal green: in Larkhall, they were always Protestant blue. Job adverts in shop windows said: "No Catholic need apply". Even at the start of the 21st century, the chemist shops put blue instead of green crosses in their windows. People elsewhere in Lanarkshire talked about Larkhall being surrounded by a metaphorical wall. It was, they said, different.

Religious bigotry was to be the least of Anne's problems. George took his new wife and daughter to live in the only place they could: the two-bedroom council house where he had grown up. They had to share it with his mother, father, brother, sister-in-law and sister. George's mother was lukewarm towards her granddaughter Isabelle. She banned Anne from the kitchen, telling her that they didn't want any of her German food. Anne, the girl who had longed to become a cookery teacher, was denied the chance to cook in the house that – and it was made most plain to her – very definitely belonged to everyone else.

George's father was a miner, slowly dying of silicosis. His brother was at that time a heavy drinker, starting on Friday night and beginning to sober up on Monday morning. His sister-in-law was an enthusiastic supporter and member of the anti-Catholic Orange

Order. The men went drinking all night in pubs with sawdust on the floors and smoked-out windows. The women stayed at home. The Falconers were a free-swearing, working-class family and none of the men wore underpants. Cheap bedspreads and other bargain items off the back of a lorry were passed around. It was a massive culture shock for the nice, middle-class German girl.

If Anne sought comfort from her husband during this period, it would have been hard for George to give. He had difficulties enough of his own. The common purpose and prestige of being a soldier was gone. He was a mere civvy in very plain clothes, trying to pick up a life he had not known since he was a boy of nineteen, some eight years before. Determined not to go down the mine, he tried his hand at becoming a bus driver, but said he had breathing difficulties with fumes from the diesel engines and had to give up. He escaped going down the pit, just. He became a coalman. Instead of hewing coal, he delivered it. George was out of the crowded house and on his lorry for most of the time.

For the only German in the town, life must have been almost unbearably lonely. The peak of misery for Anne always came in grey November, during the run-up to Armistice Day, and especially on the day itself, when the British people joined together to remember the dead of the wars. Their dead. There was no place or acknowledgement in their ceremonies and orations for Anne's own beloved brother Dieter. She cried that day in 1947 and would do so every year thereafter. She wept for her brother; perhaps she wept also for her dead Luftwaffe pilot fiancé. And perhaps too, she cried for the country she had lost and the happy life that she had never had.

As soon as she could – and it was not possible until the summer of 1950 – Anne went back to her parents and brothers in Hameln for what was understood to be a holiday. She took her toddler daughter; George stayed behind. They stayed for days, weeks, months, with an unspoken elephant of a question sitting in the Adolfstrasse living room: "When are you going back to Scotland?" The question was finally put to Anne on a late-autumn day and her answer was: "I'm not going back. I'm staying here." Her father was unbending in his response: "Go back to your husband!" he commanded. Anne had no choice but to obey.

During the next few, wretched years, the sun shone for Anne only in the summer. She made escapes for herself and little Isabelle by taking extended holidays with her parents in Hameln, vacations that lasted for ten full weeks. She got on the ferry speaking English, and got off it speaking German. Isabelle remarked: "Mum was always good at keeping her life in separate pockets."

In Hameln, pretty, vivacious Isabelle won everyone over. Minna doted on her granddaughter, taking her shopping and on expeditions to the Italian ice cream parlour. Onkel Heinrich, by now a car designer in Bremen, named the company's new model Borgward Isabella, after his niece. Cobbler Johann Kasczmarek's daughter Dagmar became Isabelle's best friend (summers only) and even Karl responded, to such an extent that Anne grumbled he showed more attention to Isabelle than he did towards his own children. Isabelle did not recall any fondness though – she remembered the grandfather of her childhood as a distant, aloof figure.

At the end of one long summer, the little girl went back to school as she always did, two weeks after her classmates. The headmistress summoned her to explain why she was so late returning to school. Isabelle chattered away, giving a full and loquacious explanation. The head stood staring at her open-mouthed. The torrent of words that poured from Isabelle was all in German. For days after every trip to the Continent, she talked nothing but German to her school-friends until she was weaned back into English.

George went to join them on their Hameln holidays once and once only. Perhaps he did not take to his in-laws or the other way round. Or maybe he simply couldn't cope for two weeks with being the only monolingual person in a house full of nattering Germans – and they included his own wife and daughter.

Isabelle's friends always marvelled at her ability to speak two languages. She looked different to her classmates too: "Children here had plain tights, but I had striped or spotted tights, because they came from Germany. When I went over, *Oma* [grandma] made my autumn and winter clothes. And at Christmas time she used to send me my summer clothes." Isabelle's outfits were all handmade by Minna and eccentrically continental as a result. But because she bore a Scottish name and spoke with a Scottish accent, the little Fräulein was never teased.

Had she been a boy, it might have been otherwise. A contemporary half-German called Charles Tamlyn, who was brought up in Cardiff, was taught to speak by his mother, who learned most of her quirky English from reading the *Western Mail* newspaper. He pleaded with his schoolfriends to play war games with the Japanese as the enemy, knowing that whenever it was Tommy against Jerry, poor Charles was always cast as the baddy.

Two things happened in the mid-1950s to ease Anne's life. The family was at last granted a council house of their own and they were able to move away from under the oppressive yoke of the Falconers. Shortly after, George's coal round took him to the town's army barracks, where he encountered a familiar accent among the housewives. He recognised the German in Mrs Eva Yarrow and suggested that she might like to meet his wife.

From then on, Friday night was German night in Larkhall. The whole Teutonic community – both of them – would sit around the dining-room table, reminiscing over tea and sandwiches, and then have fireside chats, the whole evening conducted in their native tongue.

There was a great deal of common ground in the backgrounds of the two women. Like Anne, Eva had been brought up in a Nazi household. As a little girl, Eva Mailander had been taken from the family nursery to nearby Breslau, where she was given a posy of flowers to present to the visiting Dr Goebbels. Her eldest brother died many years after the war with a copy of *Mein Kampf* on his bookshelf.

Just like Anne, Eva had a brother who was killed fighting. She vowed that if she had a son she would name the child after him. She kept her word – years later, her second child would be packed off to an English school in his lederhosen saddled with the "you're not one of us" name of Horst. At university, Horst would seek relief in anonymity by insisting that his friends call him Ed.

And like Anne, Eva endured joy and loss in a wartime engagement. She stayed in Hannover with her German fiancé's parents while he fought on the Russian front. She lived, as Anne had, through the pulverising of her adopted city by Allied air raids. Her fiancé was killed, but in a touching act of faith and loyalty on all sides, his parents became adoptive grandparents to Eva and her English husband Bob's children. Every summer, until the couple died in their nineties, Horst Yarrow and his sister Karin would go to stay with the people they cherished as *Oma* and *Opa*.

Eva had endured even worse hardships than her compatriot. After the war, she had survived on leftover beetroot and grains of wheat scratched out of the fields and had been – in her own words – "attacked by six Russians". She had fled west with her mother in a lice-ridden cattle truck crammed with refugees. And, of course, she had found and married a British soldier. The marriage did not go down well with Bob's family in England. The German army had taken off her father-in-law's arm during the Great War, so he hated her for his loss and her nationality. His daughters treated Eva likewise.

However, Eva received nothing but kindness from the people of Larkhall, and most of all from her fellow German. When Bob was injured in a car accident in which another sergeant was killed, Eva, pregnant with her first child, was shocked into premature labour. Her mother came over from Germany and Anne took Frau Mailander on the bus every day to visit the new mother and child in hospital.

For all their companionship, Eva remembered Anne most of all as a lonely person. Their friendship, an island of respite for Anne, did not last long enough. The Yarrows stayed in Larkhall for four years until Bob was posted to Burton-on-Trent. Eva experienced unpleasant discrimination there. The Falconers visited them a couple of times in faraway England and then, perhaps inevitably, the families lost touch.

By the time Anne marked ten years of living in Scotland, her native land had become a stranger to her. She scorned a new, thrusting Germany, a country she saw comprised of money-grabbing individuals seeking their fortune. At the same time, she never fully settled in Scotland. Isabelle sensed her mother's torn personality: "I don't think she ever really belonged in either country."

Anne's internal conflicts played out in her relationship with her daughter too. Isabelle always felt that her mother shielded her from the past: "She never ever spoke to me about the war. She never showed me any of the photographs. Mum always told me her father was a bank manager. I certainly didn't know my grandfather had been in a prison. I don't know whether she felt it was too much for me, on top of being different."

George was content to see his daughter happy, but as a man whose family way was to simply get by, he did not bother too much about pushing her. Anne, however, was ambitious for Isabelle, encouraging her to take the opportunities that she had been denied, to become the teacher that she had always wanted to be herself. Yet selflessness could only carry Anne so far. "I can understand her being a wee bit bitter," said Rudi. "She could hear all the others talking about what they did in their youth and she never did anything." When contemporaries reminisced about giddy nights at dance halls, Anne would say: "Dancing? What is dancing?" A life that had begun with such promise had soured into resentment and jealousy: "I can't remember her smiling at all in the last twenty, thirty years," said Isabelle. "For Mum, the glass was always half empty."

25

A little less than three years after Karl had been driven away by a US army jeep, he went back to his family in Hameln. It was unquestionably a truly momentous event for his two sons. Ten-year-old Eki had spent almost a third of his life fatherless. Rudi was just a week away from celebrating his fourteenth birthday. Some birthday present.

Neither of the boys had any recollection in later life of their father's return; Rudi did not even remember he had been away. As a man in his late seventies, he reacted with astonishment to the revelation that his father had been in prison for all of 34 months. A child psychologist offered an explanation for what appeared to be an unfathomable loss of memory. The traumatised teenager may have expunged the fact of his father's absence from his consciousness. Not one of Rudi's memories from that post-war period featured Karl, but that did not mean that at a deep level in his mind his father was not present.

Internment had worked changes in Karl. He was no longer a pudgy man, but spare, almost hollow-cheeked, and now silver-haired. There were alterations beyond the physical. Minna and her sons gathered around him to pose for photographs at Whitsun.

They looked hopefully into the camera. In every picture, Karl's face is turned away, a dead expression in his eyes. Both Rudi and Eki remembered a post-war transformation in their father: "He never was a big forceful bloke, but he was a personality," said Rudi. "After the war he was broken. You could see it when he talked; he just wasn't that interested in life."

Karl's denazification tribunal in Stade was set for July 1948. It was a small city with a big number of temporary courtrooms. Karl was allocated court number 12. In the meantime, the terms of his automatic arrest and detention meant he was barred from all employment apart from manual labour. It seemed that there wasn't even that much physical work about at that time. He spent the spring and early summer foraging in the fields and woods around Hameln, drawing on the country knowledge of his childhood to pick plants and herbs and tout them for sale to pharmacies in town. He was, quite literally, scratching a living.

A month before he went to court, the occupying powers imposed currency reforms on Germany. The savings that the family had eked out for three years were, at a stroke, almost worthless. There was no question of Karl paying a lawyer to present his case. He would have to defend himself in court.

As the date of the tribunal approached, the family grumbled about the potential make-up of those who would sit in judgment. Who, they argued, could have emerged from the war holding a position of authority, without being associated with the former regime? Their misgivings were, to some extent, justified: 71% of Lower Saxony's judges and lawyers were, at the very minimum, former members of the Nazi Party.

The family's doubts reflected a wider public disillusionment with the whole process. More than half of all Germans polled in favour of denazification in 1945: by 1948 less than a quarter supported it.

Those on the right felt it was too punitive towards "good Germans". Those on the left believed it was too lenient. All were cynical about the inevitable corruption, ineptness and evasions of a process that was overwhelmed by scale. Nearly a million Germans fell within the scope of a denazification trial. Only about a tenth of the cases actually got as far as a public hearing. The vast majority of Nazis were absolved of blame, or let off with a fine.

Karl probably travelled alone to Stade. He entered the courtroom knowing that he would be judged and classified under one of four categories:

I Major offenders (*Hauptschuldige*) – war criminals and Nazi leaders.

II Offenders (*Belastete*) – activists, militants, profiteers or incriminated persons.

III Lesser offenders (*Minderbelastete*) – those who could show mitigating circumstances, such as youth or a change of political heart at an early date.

IV Followers (*Mitläufer* – literally "one who runs alongside") – those who had only nominal involvement through party membership.

Defendants relied on presenting written sworn testimonies from friends, colleagues and neighbours giving evidence of behaviour and good character. Many were given (sometimes with the inducement of money) such a clean bill of health, such a total and improbable exoneration, that these statements were known as *Persilscheine*, (Persil documents), named after an advert for the washing powder that cleaned away brown stains.

Karl Bestle had as good as cleared the shelves: at his Dachau tribunal in March 1948, he produced no fewer than 23 squeaky-

clean statements. His neighbour Frau Babette Wagner gave a typically glowing reference: "I got to know Herr Bestle about 11 years
ago. As far as I got to know Herr Bestle in his private life, I saw
him as a quiet, hard-working and temperamentally perfect person.
During that time I did not know of him denouncing other people
and committing criminal acts." It was suspiciously similar to other
statements given on oath – ordinary Germans were processing easy
absolutions, dished out as gestures of goodwill, or solidarity, favours
that were paid for or not.

Karl's prosecutor presented his written submission before the
tribunal:

To the denazification commission in Stade

Indictment

*I hereby press (based on the Nuremberg Judgment) charges against
the civil internee, former captain of the Allgemeine and Waffen SS,*
*Karl Niemann, born 30.4.1893 in Hemeringen, Hameln, living in
Hameln, Adolfstr. 2.*

*I charge that he was after 1st Sept 1939 a member of the Allge-
meine and Waffen SS, even though he knew that the aforementioned
organisation was used for perpetrating acts that (according to article
VI of the International Military Court) are considered as crimes,
and are described as punishable according to the Nuremberg Judgment.*

Essential reason for suspicion:

*The defendant was after 1st Sept 1939 a member of an organisa-
tion that the Nuremberg Judgment declares criminal. He knew that*

---

* The SS was divided into the *Allgemeine* (general or civil) and *Waffen* (military
– the word *Waffen* means weapons).

*the aforementioned organisation was used for committing acts that,
in the sense of the Nuremberg Judgment, are crimes.*

Herr RA Beier

Stade

Ritterstr. 13

I request oral proceedings.

a) Crimes against peace

*Planning, preparation, beginning and carrying out an offensive
war or a war that violates international contracts, treaties, or assurances, or the participation in a complicit plan, or conspiracy in order
to perform one of the above.*

b) War crimes

*Violation of the law and the use of war. To these violations belong
the following acts, but the term should not be limited to them,
namely the killing or abuse of members of the civil population of an
occupied area, or the deportation of civilians from occupied areas for
slave labour or other purposes, the killing, abuse of war prisoners,
or people on the sea, the killing of hostages, looting of private and
public properties, deliberate destruction of cities, districts, or villages,
or devastation that are not justified by military necessity.*

c) Crimes against humanity

*Murder, eradication, deportation, mutilation, or other inhumane
actions that were committed before or during a war against any civil
population, or persecution for political, racial, or religious reasons
[the rest of this section is illegible]*

*The defendant became a member of the NSDAP on 1.1.1931 and
was from 1932 to 1935 cell leader. From 1.11.1935, he belonged
to the Allgemeine SS, where he reached the rank of captain. In
1935, he became an auditor for the economic enterprises of the SS in
Dachau. From there, he was transferred in 1938 to the Business and
Administration Main Office of the SS in Berlin, where he worked as*

auditor, as the chair of the department, and eventually as the deputy acting director in office W4. This office was mainly responsible for wood and metal processing factories (DAW), which were all located in close proximity to concentration camps and in which camp prisoners were employed. In 1942, he was transferred to the Waffen SS. He retained, however, his position in the WVHA, and was registered there as a captain.

The aims of the NSDAP and the tasks of the SS were well known to the defendant because of his year-long membership, his education, and his work as a cell leader of the NSDAP, and as a deputy acting director of the WVHA. Because of these circumstances, it is, despite his denial, to be assumed that he knew of the atrocities committed by the SS in the camps. This is also because in addition, he interacted with SS members and personnel of the office group D (whose responsibility was the administration of the camps), and met and dealt with prisoners in the factories of the DAW, for years. At least he knew, as he confessed, that political opponents of the Nazis, Bible researchers,* clergymen and Jews were without judicial judgment imprisoned (by the Gestapo) in the camps (of which the defendant knew a great number), and held there for uncertain time, stripped of their freedom and forced into hard labour. Because he also knew that the camps were guarded by, and controlled by the SS, he knew the use of the SS for the crimes against humanity. He finally knew of the racial persecution under National Socialism to the extent that he heard of the transport of the Jews to the east.

By being and remaining a member of the Allgemeine and Waffen SS, the defendant supported these organisations in their criminal acts and contributed to the violation of basic principles of humanity and the damaging of the reputation of the German people.

---

* A catch-all phrase that includes, primarily, Jehovah's Witnesses.

The text highlights both the strengths and weaknesses of the prosecution case. Denazification prosecutors were invariably hampered by the disinclination of Germans to speak out to condemn their fellow citizens. Denunciation was something that had been feared and denigrated in the Nazi era. Morally, it had been a suspect thing to do. Prosecutor Baier had no personal testimony at his disposal to incriminate Karl.

What he did have in his favour was the sheer weight of circumstantial evidence. The Pohl trial at Nuremberg had established a legal precedent that, without doubt, the offices of the WVHA had ordered and committed atrocities. Even if it proved impossible, through lack of evidence, to show *how* defendants had acted as individuals, their managerial roles within those offices proved culpability. In effect, they were being judged as representatives of their function. All Prosecutor Baier had to do was to follow the precedent, to lay out Karl's Nazi pedigree, proof of affiliation and support for the regime, and then let the case rest on his position as a manager of the WVHA.

Karl offered sworn testimonies from camp inmates in evidence. There was, of course, Müller-Strobl, whose statement included the affirmation that:

> *From 1942–1945, I was in permanent contact with him, and I can only say one thing about him: Herr Niemann wrote uncountable release requests for political prisoners. Some of them then became full-paid free employees of the factories that they had worked for [as prisoners]. These people and I owe Herr Niemann our freedom.*

Hamburg man Friedrich Naupold had given his gushing testimony (see page 105) in a surfeit of exclamation marks. Was there any reason why he should lie?

Karl Steiner, writing as owner of the firm "Barock" Salzburg, had declared in his letter to Mimi Schmidt:

Your uncle was truly a helpful, friendly man who was always benevolent towards us prisoners when he visited Dachau.

I can very well remember that Herr Niemann made an effort to get me released. He requested (at the Reich Security Main Office) that I should work for him. Yet, in my case, all efforts were in vain.

Franz Doppler, by then a professor at the Institute of Engineering Technology in Vienna, stated:

…even at the SS economic administration main office in Berlin, where I had to appear, no one could tell me about the precise circumstances surrounding my release from Dachau in Aug 1942. Hence I unfortunately do not know to what extent Herr Niemann was involved.

I don't wish to omit, however, the positive note that in the DAW in the Dachau camp, the name of (the then chief clerk) Herr Niemann was well known among the prisoners. I never heard that Herr Niemann's name was mentioned in connection with measures that were detrimental to the prisoners.

Walter Koch, a fellow internee at Moosburg, vouchsafed that:

…the former camp prisoners Müller-Strobl (at this time in Dachau concentration camp) and Siebold (at this time in Buchenwald) were, on request of Karl Niemann, in his job as manager of the DAW Berlin, released from their camps and simultaneously became civil employees for the firm. They were therewith on equal terms with all the other civil employees, and were used according to their strength and knowledge.

There was even a joint statement from three civilians who had worked at the pig and poultry farm at Dachau training camp in the late 1930s, who testified: "The farm was at that time controlled and managed by Herr Karl Niemann, born 30.4.93 in Hemeringen, Hameln district. Along with us civil workers, there were also camp prisoners (15–20 men). Because of an order by the above-mentioned person, they were always treated humanely. We do not know of incidents of any kind."

Karl had few sworn testimonies that were scrubbed with *Persilscheine*. Only the daughter of his former landlady and his former Dachau landlord may have fallen into that category. Anneliese Präel wrote:

I know Herr Niemann as a dutiful and industrious man with a calm, objective character. An exceptional family life made the time spent in the home of the Niemann family a pleasure. Herr Niemann never expressed himself politically in private and was never propagandistically active. His wife was/is completely apolitical, and his children were only politically organised to the extent that this was necessary. These are facts that show that Herr Niemann was not a fanatic. Herr Niemann was known for his helpful character. It has never come to my ears that he harmed someone; rather he was always concerned about helping others wherever possible. I also could never observe that he used his position for personal advantages.

I am not related by blood or marriage to Niemann. I have never belonged to the party. It is known to me that these statements will be presented to the denazification committee, and that the provision of any false information will be punishable.

Karl's Dachau landlord Martin Weinsteiger declared: "Herr Karl Niemann was from 1935–1938 one of my quietest and most pleasant tenants. In interactions with my family, the house inhabitants, the neighbourhood and me, he always exhibited a peaceful, noble character. He never placed his political views or his rank into the foreground."

If events in Bavaria were anything to go by, Karl needed a strong defence. His fellow SS manager, Karl Bestle, who in many respects had followed the same career path, had been placed by the Dachau tribunal in the second-highest category of offender. Bestle was judged to have been a *Belastete*, an activist offender, and was punished accordingly. He was sentenced to one and a half years in jail (which he had already served), given a whopping fine of 11,700 marks and subjected to heavy restrictions, including being banned from public office, belonging to a trade union, professional organisation or political party, or being employed in business or as a teacher, preacher, editor or writer for a period of five years. Bestle promptly hired a lawyer and began to mount an appeal.

The only record of Karl Niemann's performance in court that day lies within the judgment. After he had stood up to give his defence, the court retired and the panel of four men considered both written and oral evidence. They gave their verdict against the bank clerk and former captain of the Allgemeine and Waffen SS (reproduced in full in the Appendix on page 263). It provides a fascinating insight into arguments and counter-arguments, the prosecution case and Karl's attempts at justifying or absolving himself of blame.

The presiding judge, Herr Schulz, began by summarising Karl's career and came down in favour of a presumption made by the prosecution:

It is clear that the defendant had been since 1.11.35 a member of the

Allgemeine SS (and in the end held the rank of SS captain) and since
1942 a member of the Waffen SS. He belongs therefore to a group
of people who count as criminals (according to … the Nuremberg
Judgment).

Judge Schulz set out the case, beyond reasonable doubt, that Karl
was aware of the illegality and mistreatment of inmates:

The defendant knew of most of the concentration camps from his
own experience. While working in Dachau from 1935–1938,
he watched the camp prisoners at work. He also did so while he
was a member of the WVHA and on numerous business trips…
to the concentration camps of Auschwitz, Buchenwald, Dachau,
Lemberg, Lublin, Neuengamme, Ravensbrück, Sachsenhausen
and Stutthof. He saw and talked to the prisoners there. He knew
that in these camps were primarily political prisoners who were
active against the regime, and that a smaller number of inmates
were professional criminals, anti-social elements, Bible researchers
and persons who violated article 175 of the German Penal Code.
He knew that some of the political opponents were only impris-
oned there because of their political convictions. The same applied
to Jews, who were often only arrested because of their race… The
defendant had knowledge that the incarceration happened in most
cases without judicial judgment…

Schulz presented evidence that Karl knew of atrocities, and
included one bizarre piece of Karl's reasoning concerning coffins:

The fatalities in Dachau concentration camp were, according to his
knowledge, about fifteen per quarter year. He said he found this out
by the number of coffins that were made. He said he never heard

about facilities in the camps for cremating people or about gas chambers. He said he did not know of the "special treatment"* and executions of prisoners, or … about medical experiments on prisoners.

He knew that most of those who were sent to camps were there without any assurance of an orderly judicial process, and thereby lost their freedom for years and became exposed to the despotism of the camp leader and the camp guards.

Even if the defendant did indeed not know about the atrocities such as the hanging, the gassing, the executions by firing squad, he still knew according to his own confessions about the inhumane treatment of the camp prisoners, in particular about the fact that beatings were used not only as a disciplinary measure and that prisoners had to work with insufficient food until exhaustion.

Perhaps the most intriguing and perplexing part of the whole judgment lies in the next paragraph:

The defendant was fully aware of the injustice of these measures because he did not deny his own responsibility from the beginning. He also confessed that he did reflect on the whole system of the camps, but suggested that if he had said or done something, he would possibly have been sent to a camp himself. But he did not explain why, given his knowledge about all this, he had never had any wish to withdraw from his organisation.

Schulz goes on to pick up on this last point:

The assumption of distress is out of the question; because the defendant did not show any evidence that after recognising the injustice

---

* The German word used was *Sonderbehandlung*, a Nazi euphemism for killing.

of the camps, he was in psychological conflict and thus felt the moral duty to withdraw from the organisation.

The name of Auschwitz hangs unsaid in the next statement. There was an assumption that no defendant could claim ignorance of atrocities if they had been there. Even Kommandant Höss freely stated that there was a permanent stench of burning bodies lingering over the camp. Nothing could be proved:

The submission by the defendant that he visited Lemberg and Lublin only briefly a few times, and apart from that never spent time in occupied areas in the east and thus did not know anything about the mass executions of the Jews in the east could not be contradicted in the oral proceedings.

The weight of evidence then began to shift as Schulz presented mitigating factors:

The prisoners' declarations and police reports from Dachau and Dortmund show that his personal behaviour was impeccable, and that he was not politically active. The declarations of four former camp prisoners speak particularly in the defendant's defence. ... Doppler ... had never heard about the defendant being involved in anything harmful to the prisoners ... the defendant was called "Papa Niemann" by prisoners in Sachsenhausen because of his benevolent behaviour and willingness to help. ... Political prisoners... owe their freedom to the defendant.

And so Schulz concluded:

The behaviour of the defendant allows the conclusion that despite his constant contact with the camps, he remained a humane person. According to Müller-Strobl, he had already realised back then that the camp system would lead to the downfall of the German people.

Furthermore, because the defendant also did not make an unfavourable impression in oral proceedings and also overall held to the truth, a prison term of one year as atonement appears – despite his extensive knowledge of the system of the camps and in consideration of his tolerant behaviour towards the prisoners – to be sufficient and apt.

According to ... the Code of Criminal Procedure, the time already spent in prison is counted towards the sentence, and the length of this time already fully offsets the sentence.

Karl walked out of the court a free man. He had been classified as a Follower (*Mitläufer*), the lowest grade of offender, officially "an opportunist who had joined Nazi organisations but not participated in their activities". This was patently not true and, to many eyes, it would appear that he had got off extremely lightly. But for whatever reason, Karl did not accept his punishment. He appealed against the court's judgment. Perhaps he was banking on being given a smaller fine. Or maybe he thought he was not guilty of anything at all.

26

There was nothing for it but to look for a job. The verdict meant that – until his appeal – he could only do manual labour. There were labouring jobs to be had… but it meant swallowing a great deal of pride. Karl went to the enemy and got work as a labourer for the British army's Royal Engineers. He worked on the army training ground, sometimes sweeping up, often dragging heavy floating pontoons around. For a man heading into his late fifties, who had spent a lifetime doing no more exercise than pushing pieces of paper around a desk, it was physically draining.

Karl never complained, but instead told his children about the kindness shown to him by soldiers less than half his age, who liked the willing, but visibly worn-out older man: "The British soldiers didn't overdo it with him. If they thought something was too much for him, they'd say 'take it easy, Karl, take it easy. I'll do that – you leave it,'" said Rudi.

Eki paints a picture of a pathetic figure: "I still see Vati now, as he was at that time, tired and struggling with work. An old army bag over his shoulder, he had to go the whole way from the army training ground on foot every day, because there were hardly any buses and then they were too dear. It must all have been very hard and humiliating."

Autumn came, and impecunious, nicotine-addicted Karl sat in his back yard with an old schoolteacher chum, Otto Kallmeyer, staring at the tobacco plants he had planted that spring, watching the leaves turn yellow, hoping that they would bring a harvest. He also pressed for his appeal to be heard in his home town. On 23rd September 1948, he wrote to the main denazification committee of Hameln: "I ask that my case be put through as soon as possible, so that I have the possibility of making a return to my skilled occupation as a businessman. Currently, I am working as a labourer at the Scharnhorst barracks."

The legal process dragged on through the winter and into the following spring. Karl sent an indignant response to the case laid out against him by the prosecuting counsel, which had recommended – as the Stade prosecutor had recommended – for Karl to be placed in the category of Minor Offender. He answered:

In response to the motion by the public prosecutor from 24.3.49, I hereby submit the following counter-statement: from the material that I submitted, the prosecutor selected randomly dates and events to prove that I was strongly active in support of National Socialism. Against the claims the prosecutor made, I note:

My full-time work at the DAF in the years 1934/35 was the result of a dilemma. As chairman at the firm F.R. Wilh. Ruhfus in Dortmund, I was forced to put an end to the tariff-less state of about 150 employees. The consequence was that it became impossible for me to stay at the firm. Through my move to the DAF, my income sank from 500 RM to 220 RM.

In the years 1935–38, I was an auditor for the economic enterprises of the SS in Dachau, which were under the control of the SS

Munich, and not, as it is claimed, under the control of the concen-
tration camp. Thus the claim that after my probation at the camp I
went as an SS captain and deputy acting director of the Business and
Administration Main Office to Berlin no longer applies. In 1938,
I was second lieutenant of the SS. I became captain of the SS in
1940, and acting director in 1943. My annual income in Dachau
was about 6,000 RM. Not until 1945 did I reach one of 13,200.
With respect to the release of prisoners that I engaged in, I refer in
this regard to the enclosed copy of the judgment by the denazification
court, Stade, in which this question is dealt with extensively and
judicially.

Karl Niemann

As a determined rebuttal of the case against him, it was no more
than a quibbling over minor detail. He had no substantial argument
to swing things in his favour.

On a May morning, Karl crossed the Weser to attend the tribunal
appeal in the courtroom of the *Hochzeitshaus* – the town wedding
building. As before, he was without a defence lawyer and stood to
present his evidence before the judge and a panel of five arbitra-
tors. The outcome was predictable. As before, he was branded as a
Follower, the lowest category of offender. In summing up, the judge
remarked, with words that caught the prevailing political wind:

In recognition of the convincing evidence for his defence, the
committee refrained from classifying him as belonging to group III
[as a minor offender]. The committee was convinced that the person
concerned has the honest will to get in line with German democracy.
The committee takes into account his political burden by recognising
his claim that he was unable to choose.

Karl's performance in court that day had not gone unnoticed. There were those in attendance who told him that his defence had been so convincing that he should defend others who stood accused. In the gallery was a journalist from the local paper. Karl spoke afterwards of how the reporter had approached him, congratulated him on an eloquent, persuasive case and then offered him a job on the paper. Because of his criminal conviction, Karl was barred from taking up the offer. And he had no money to pay his fine – even though it was just twenty marks. Rudi had not long been confirmed in the church and had been given gifts and money to mark the occasion: "All of the money was taken away to pay for my father's denazification. I was told that someone – a concentration camp inmate – stood up in court and said my father was the only person who treated him like a human being. That was my father. He would never have hurt anyone."

If the Hameln journalist ever wrote up the story, the case never appeared in print. For a start, far bigger things were now happening outside the town, events that would occupy acres of local newsprint. In the very week of Karl's tribunal, a law was passed to create a new Federal Republic of Germany. The papers deliberated over the meanings of words such as "democracy" and "social responsibility" enshrined in the proposed constitution. Approved by the Allies and enacted by the end of the month, it promised a new beginning, unity in a country now divided. West Berlin sat as an island in a sea of Russian-dominated and partitioned East Germany. A few weeks later, Stalin would launch a blockade, an unsuccessful attempt to starve the Allies out of the old capital.

A more compelling reason for Karl's case being unreported was the probability that nobody wanted to read about it. The new chancellor of West Germany, Konrad Adenauer, gave his first speech to the new *Bundestag* (parliament) on 20th September 1949. It included a telling sentence: "The government of the Federal Republic, in the belief that many have atoned for a guilt that was subjectively not heavy, is determined where it appears acceptable to put the past behind us."

Local historian Bernhard Gelderblom captures the prevailing mood in Hameln at that time: "The town did not speak about its Nazi past. The subject was taboo. The general opinion was that they wanted to draw a line; not to look back but to build Hameln again. The expression was 'Schwamm drüber!' – sponge it away."

Former Nazis eased back into positions of authority. Hans Krüger, a stormtrooper in 1933, had been an officer in The Office of Racial Policy of the party and gave talks on racial defilement. As a town official, he was primarily responsible for evicting the town's Jews from their homes, packing them into hideously overcrowded houses, liquidating their assets and arranging for their deportation to concentration camps. After the war, and following denazification and categorisation as a Follower, he slipped back into his old job. A Jew was asking for redress after losing his home and furniture. The decision fell to Krüger. He found against the appellant.

Under the new regime and its relaxed attitudes towards former Nazis, Karl tried to resurrect his career. He wrote to his old employer, the Deutsche Bank. The reply was succinct and negative: "Too old". The British army, however, realised that his talents were wasted in the open air, and moved him out of labouring into office work. Whether they knew his background or not, it became an irrelevance to them. Eki said: "His 'English employer' was very tolerant and humane with Vati."

During this period, Karl may have read in the paper news of his old bosses – that they had been hanged. Oswald Pohl went to the gallows in June 1951. Gerhard Maurer went the same way four weeks before Karl's 60th birthday. Maurer had employed two of

Germany's best lawyers for his defence. They drew testimony in Maurer's favour from both Müller-Strobl and Franz Doppler. Being nice to a couple of Austrians was not enough to atone for working hundreds of thousands of Jews to their deaths. A Polish court found him guilty.

The two boys grew up in total ignorance of what had gone before. "The Nazis were never spoken about either at home or at school," said Eki. "I think nobody wanted to hear or say anything about it." Rudi recalled the absurdity of history lessons: "We were taught about the ancient Greeks and the Romans. Nothing more recent than that." A whole generation forgot everything and the next one learned nothing.

Minna was trapped in what is called by psychologists ambiguous loss. She grieved for Dieter, but since his body had not been found, she clung to very slim hopes that he might be alive. She wrote to the missing persons' authorities who were cooperating with the German Red Cross to trace lost soldiers from the war. No letter with news of his fate came back in her lifetime.

However, during the 1950s, Minna enjoyed something of a personal renaissance. She moved comfortably into the role of neighbourhood sage that her father had held in Adolfstrasse before her. The next generation of puzzled and confused Hameliners would come to her door, asking her to explain or fill in official forms for them, or give advice. She went to college to begin the dressmaking apprenticeship she had missed in her youth: "After so many weeks she said: 'I can do it myself, I don't have to go for an apprenticeship,'" said Rudi. "So she stopped and she made me a suit. A knickerbocker suit. When she got a pattern, she never cut it the way they said. She cut it to get maximum material, minimum effort, and it worked out fine."

For Minna's sons, there was no possibility – at that time – of either of them going to university, for there wasn't enough money coming into the house. Both took tradesman's apprenticeships, Rudi as a toolmaker. His achievements as a young adult were unspectacular, unless you count cycling the entire length of the country with a guitar on his back to camp at the Bodensee (Lake Constance). And then there was the story of the sharpshooter…

"What happened, when I was serving my time [as an apprentice toolmaker], I went and bought myself a starting pistol. I cut the barrel off, made up a new barrel, screwed it in, so I had a 2.2 pistol. You could get ammunition, no bother, but not a pistol. But I managed it, so I got myself a packet of ammunition. And then I went down to the water, to the river. Well, there was nobody else around, I thought. I put pieces of wood up and then Bang! Bang, bang! After a while I was getting fed up so I went home. And then my mother, she said: 'Did you hear that? There was some idiot down at the river shooting pistols!' And I said: 'Was there?'"

At sixteen, Eki left school to begin his apprenticeship as an interior decorator. He was also a national canoeing champion. A dashing, good-looking young man posed for his church confirmation in the suit that Dieter had worn before him. On a rare outing through Hameln, his elder brother pointed out that every girl in town was following them. "They're all after you." "Are they?" replied the pied piper of Fräuleins in all innocence.

As for Karl, he worked on quietly at his desk as a British army administrator for the rest of his career. Eki commented that "He was released into retirement at the age of 65 with regrets and respect."

27

A road to the east opened up in the mid-1950s. Though effectively under Russian control, the Deutsche Demokratische Republik (DDR) began to accept applications from the refugees who had fled westwards at the end of the war to return to East Germany and reclaim the goods and chattels they had left behind. During the long summer of 1954 in Hameln, Anne urged her mother to apply to the authorities. A request went in to the notoriously labyrinthine bureaucracy of Berlin; a year later it spat out an affirmative answer.

There was no question of Karl going to his former home in Berlin – he was banned for life from crossing any national border. At nearly 60 years of age, Minna volunteered to take on the job. The family could not afford to hire a removal van, but they knew a butcher who would rent out a truck and trailer, together with a driver – himself. The two parties agreed a fee of 500 Deutschmarks and so Minna and her butcher-chauffeur set off towards the Harz mountains and the East German border in a not entirely trustworthy vehicle that had seen better days during or even before the war.

Ten years since she had left Dienstweg 19 under very different circumstances, Minna returned to her old home. Though the street had changed its name to Heppenheimer Weg, the houses looked just the same. Minna walked up to the doorstep and knocked on the front door. A woman answered. Her name was Frau Schwartz. Things did not go at all well. Minna explained that she had come to collect her furniture and other possessions and that she had official sanction to do so. The woman let her in, but her manner bordered on open hostility. Frau Schwartz had known Minna was coming and knew why. Perhaps she resented having to surrender the furniture in a house she had moved into after the war fully furnished. It had been the only furnished house in the street and she and her husband had had none at that time. There would have been another, deeper reason for her barely contained dislike. After the war, victims of the Nazi regime had been encouraged to move into the Zehlendorf estate. Frau Schwartz was Jewish.

In the downstairs hall, Frau Schwartz pointed to the wall and said contemptuously: "You had a big picture of Hitler here." "Of course," Minna remonstrated. "Everyone had to have a picture of Hitler in their house. You had to." "And what about these…?" asked Frau Schwartz, jabbing her finger accusingly at invisible rectangles on the wall surrounding the imaginary portrait. "My husband's certificates. For promotions, long service, that kind of thing," answered Minna. In the most bizarre circumstances, she was defending Karl as if he were simply the loyal company man.

In the dining room, there was no sign of Frederick the Great, the generals or the mounted Hussar. All of Karl's precious (and by now valuable) porcelain had disappeared. Minna did not ask where it had gone. Frau Schwartz led Minna down the steep steps to the cellar. Minna remembered turning the corner and looking into the back room and seeing that the wooden bunk beds, where the family had sheltered at first from the bombs, were still in place. Then the frosty-faced woman took Minna upstairs to the bedroom where all the furniture was stacked.

The butcher-removal man began to carry the furniture out to the van – the four carved oak chairs, the great table, the wardrobe, a few other items, with Minna perhaps helping where she could. Then, as the room emptied, Frau Schwartz's mood changed inexplicably. She gestured to a long sewing box. "Do you not want to take this with you? Please do." Minna was swayed a little by her sudden but welcome thaw and her importunate attitude. The sewing box was loaded into the truck and the two women parted with a semblance of amicability.

The truck drove on towards the Russian border point and Minna sat uneasily, sensing something was not right. Before they came to the checkpoint, she made her driver stop and open the trailer at the back of the truck. She lifted the lid of the sewing box that Frau Schwartz had been so insistent she take, pulled out the contents and found a gun concealed at the bottom of the box. It was the hunting rifle that Karl had been given by the state for his 50th birthday. Had the Russians found it, Minna and the butcher would not have been returning to Hameln for a very long time, if at all.

And indeed, the two travellers only just made it back to Hameln. The laden old vehicle rattled and clanked all the way through East Germany, over the border and through Brunswick. The moment it juddered to a halt outside the house in Adolfstrasse, its front axle snapped and the truck collapsed on the road. Teenage Eki came out to help unload the stricken vehicle, carting its contents into the yard at the back of the house. They tipped the table on its top and that was when Eki saw it – a swastika and the words *Deutsche Ausrüstungswerke** branded on the underside. If the Russians or the *Vopos* (the Volkspolizei – the East German police) had discovered it at the border, they would have been very very interested to learn more.

---

*   The SS company of which Karl was a manager.

Before long, the bulk of the furniture was shipped in a container to Anne in Scotland and, for the rest of her life, the table and chairs and the great wardrobe stood in her living room. Isabelle had no recollection of seeing swastikas under the table, or any writing at all. Maybe someone had rather prudently got to work with a sander before it left Germany.

28

University had always been Rudi's long-term goal. When his toolmaking apprenticeship came to an end after three years, he planned to earn enough money to fund a degree in mechanical engineering. Somehow he found out that he could earn much more in his sister's adopted country than he could in his homeland. The family agreed that he should go to Larkhall for two years, a long enough time to pay for a degree at university – Munich maybe, or perhaps Stuttgart. Minna would accompany her son and stay for a few weeks – it would be the first trip abroad for both of them.

In June 1956, mother and son travelled in the *Flying Scotsman* from London up to Glasgow. The train made a stop at a station on the way and Minna told Rudi to speak to the guard on the platform, to ask him a question. Rudi was too frightened to say anything. He had only learned English for a year or so at school. He was only too glad to reach Larkhall and hide in his sister's house.

Three weeks into Minna's holiday in Scotland, George suggested that the visitors might like to sample some of the local culture. On one of those rare sunny July days, he took them down to Springburn in Glasgow and they stood in a crowd outside a cinema, where Gina Lollobrigida was starring in *The World's Most Beautiful Woman*.

Some kind of parade was in progress. A band marched past playing pipes, flutes and drums. Men carried banners and flags. For Minna, the parade might have evoked memories of Dortmund or Berlin under the Nazis. As for Rudi: "It was very interesting but I didn't have a clue what was going on." The new arrivals were witnessing an Orange Lodge parade,* a sectarian march through the city.

The time came for Minna to go home. A 61-year-old woman returning alone from her first visit to a foreign country, she made her way back to Germany and arrived at a station 30 miles from Hameln, where Eki had arranged to collect her. There was some mix-up and Eki arrived several hours late. He found his mother sitting on the platform untroubled, knitting a pullover.

In Larkhall, Rudi shared a bedroom with his nine-year-old niece for more than two and a half years. He slept in the single bed that Anne had had brought over from Hameln the year before. Isabelle remembered her uncle: "headstrong and opinionated, just like his sister".

Rudi was no longer a tourist, but an immigrant. For a while, he was bewildered by the Lanarkshire accents around him: "Everyone could understand me. But I couldn't understand a word they were saying." He found Scottish eating habits peculiar too. A boy who had known years of hunger was mystified by the strange rituals: "When I came to this country I thought it was customary to leave something behind on the plate after a meal, because it always happened wherever I was – one potato, or even half a potato. To me, it seemed such a waste."

He went to the police station and signed the Aliens Register.

---

* Orange parades are held around 12th July to mark the Battle of the Boyne of 1690, when troops under Protestant William of Orange defeated a Catholic army in Ireland.

While he waited for a work permit, he tagged along in his brother-in-law's lorry as the coalman's assistant. In those days, people kept coal in the house, so he was often carrying heavy sacks up staircases to tip them out in an upstairs flat. Hard labour, but he enjoyed it. He never got on terribly well with his employer and brother-in-law, though, and once played a prank out of boredom and frustration in which he hopped into the driver's seat and drove away while George was chatting at length to one of his customers.

Moonlighting Rudi was hauled over the coals by the police. Someone must have shopped him: the police stopped the lorry and asked if he had authorisation to work. Rudi's halting English gave him the perfect cover. He told them he was only there to learn the language. Either they believed him or they felt it was too much trouble to stumble through mutual incomprehension and take it any further.

When his work permit came through, Rudi applied for the job of toolmaker at an engineering company in nearby Motherwell. The foreman began the interview with a key question that tested Rudi's suitability for the post:

"What religion are you?"

"Lutheran."

"A whit?"

Some careful negotiation established that Rudi was some kind of Proddy and "no a Kaflik". The foreman continued pursuing his important line of inquiry:

"Let us say that at the end of the week you have a wee bit of cash left over. Would you give it to the Orange Lodge?"

"No, I bloody wouldn't!" replied the young German, who had learned a few very useful words of English.

A qualified and much-needed toolmaker, Rudi got the job and, with one exception, found nothing but friendliness in his workplace. The exceptional individual sneered: "I hate Germans" and told Rudi during the run-up to Remembrance Sunday: "You shouldnae be allowed tae wear a poppy." Nobody else said anything offensive: "They might have thought it, but they did not tell me." Many men in the factory believed there was a greater enemy than the one who had spent six years not so long ago trying to kill them. Rudi could have been English.

Fair-haired, wearing horn-rimmed spectacles and a stick-up haircut that made him the Rick Astley of the 50s, Rudi zipped around town on a scooter. George warned him against it, telling him that it was too soon, that he was not sufficiently familiar with British roads. Rudi paid no heed. "He was a menace on that bike!" said Isabelle. A greater menace in a car raced out of a side street onto the main road one day without looking or stopping. Rudi was thrown into the air, his kneecap was shattered, he lost his hearing in one ear and spent days unconscious in hospital. Both his brother and sister said the accident changed his personality. The reckless car driver was summoned to court. On the day of his trial, nothing happened. The young man had been the son of an important local figure. At the last minute, without giving any explanation, the police dropped the charges.

Rudi had more than just his sister to nurse him back to health. He had met a Glaswegian typist with a mass of curly brown hair at a dance hall – the dating venue of the time par excellence. May Coulter was drawn to the faintly exotic man who was "not like Scottish boys". Rudi toured her relations and endeared himself to them with party tricks – he was a Mr Fixer, whose practical nous enabled him to mend the broken and damaged.

The couple were on the verge of becoming engaged when May's father sat her down for a heart-to-heart talk. Willie Coulter was a fair and broad-minded man who – to use a familiar phrase – took people as he found them and never said a bad word about anybody. Many years later, he would urge his daughter to leave Scotland so that her sons would not be tainted by religious bigotry. That day, he raised doubts about their marriage, not on the basis of Rudi's personality, but of his nationality. Germany had started two wars in his lifetime. Was his daughter sure she could take the risk of marrying someone whose country might start another and divide the nations? May took the risk: they married in March 1959.

When Rudi left Germany in 1956, he had promised his younger brother that he would earn enough to pay for Eki to buy a driving licence. It never happened. Siblings have long memories.

29

In the last summer of their lives, Karl and Minna sat round a table in a leafy Hameln beer garden. White-haired Karl now had a stick and sat awkwardly in the manner of an elderly man for whom movement was difficult. Minna, a little stout, had tight grey curls. Though 63 years of age, she looked appreciably older. A smiling well-tanned contemporary was at the table with them, a moustached man holding a cigar, wearing a waistcoat, cap and a decidedly loud tie. The occasion was captured by a photographer. Another chair, pushed back from the table, hinted that the photographer was one of the group.

Neither Rudi nor Eki could identify the man in the picture. There is nothing exceptional in that – parents have friends whom their children will not necessarily know, never mind recognise. Yet at the same time, neither son could explain how, when the printed photograph was turned over, it bore the name of a developer far far away – *Peter Roth, Schliersee*.

At that time of their lives, Karl and Minna were in no fit state to make a long journey down to the Alpine town where Karl had been arrested. So had Schliersee come to them? In post-war years, the resort became a focus for an annual gathering of the right-wing

Freikorps Oberland, a notorious outfit that had included among its members Heinrich Himmler, the *Kommandants* of both Dachau and Gross-Rosen and one Karl Bestle. It was the kind of place where an old Nazi would settle and fit in very comfortably. Was this cheery figure Bestle, or another of Karl's former SS associates, paying him a visit from Bavaria, and then sending him a picture of the occasion as a memento?

Nineteen fifty-nine was the year in which both of Karl's sons were married and Eki's first son was born. It was also the year when Karl's wife and children saw his personality melt away as dementia took hold. Rudi and May went to Hameln after their wedding and found Karl operating in automatic: "Mutti would say – 'Karl, wash the potatoes!' and he would go to the sink and wash the potatoes. 'Karl, chop the carrots!' She would give him a knife and chopping board and he would chop the carrots." For the rest of the day, Karl would sit silently in his chair in the corner under the last picture of his dead son, his mouth fixed in a watery smile, eyes gazing into nothingness.

Isabelle celebrated her twelfth birthday on 5th February 1960. She rushed home from school, only to be greeted with the news that her grandfather had died. Anne and Rudi travelled to Hameln for the funeral. Anne was still there when her mother had a stroke. She went to see her in hospital and told Isabelle much later that her gravely ill and perhaps confused mother had said hurtful things. Anne may not have understood that a stroke sufferer with a damaged brain can speak out of character. And this would have been completely out of character. The hurtful words were a cruel final injustice meted out on a loyal daughter.

Most of all, Minna told Anne that she did not want to live any longer without Karl. Her plea was answered very quickly. The doctors told her that she had to stay in bed for the sake of her heart.

Minna got up and tried walking down the corridor. She did so again and again. Nineteen days after her husband's death, Minna suffered a fatal heart attack.

Well over three years after the couple's deaths, a letter arrived at Adolfstrasse addressed to Frau Wilhelmine Niemann. It was opened by her brother Willi, the last surviving member of the Schwenker family:

Dear Frau Niemann

The search service of the German Red Cross, with whom we work in the field of missing persons investigations, has sent us your "registered missing in the Federal Republic" search request. We see from this that your son Dietrich Niemann, born on 23rd January 1926 in Hameln, was reported for the last time in Erlangen on 28th March 1945.

From the municipality of Iffigheim, postal district Sensheim in Kitzingen, Lower Franconia, we have received the message that a Wehrmacht soldier is buried in Iffigheim cemetery, whose identification tag was marked "- 13418 - Stm.Kp.Pz.Ers.Abt . 5".

This soldier died in Iffigheim on 4th/5th April 1945. More details about the death are not known here.

In the copies of our available dog tag directories of the former Wehrmacht it was discovered that your son Dietrich Niemann, born on 01.23.1926, was the bearer of this identification tag.

We regret to inform you of this sad news at this time and do not want to fail to express our condolences.

For a report on the situation, the state of the grave and a possible visit to the cemetery, we recommend that you apply to the German War Graves Commission, Luther Place, Kassel.

In order to instigate civil certification, we ask you to complete the enclosed personnel questionnaire and return it to us, and we thank you for your efforts in advance.

Yours faithfully
Kirchhoff

German service (WASt) for notification to next of kin of fallen soldiers of the former German Wehrmacht.

Minna's brother Willi did the German thing of obeying officialdom and wrote back the same day. Thereafter, Anne and her brothers did nothing. They all had children to care for and they looked to the future, not the past: "Mutti was gone; what was there left for us to do?" shrugged Eki. None of them ever went to visit Dieter's grave.

Eight young men are buried together in a plot at Iffigheim cemetery, identifiable only by their names and places of birth. No regiments, no political affiliations. *Ernst-Dietrich Niemann, aus Hameln* is the fourth name listed. There is a memorial tablet with an inscription:

Im Kampf um Iffigheim am 5 April 1945 fielen acht Deutsche Soldaten. Sie sind auf diesem Friedhof zur letzten Ruhe gebettet.

In the battle for Iffigheim on 5th April 1945, fell eight German soldiers. They were laid in this cemetery as their last resting place.

Endlich

Decades after the war had ended, a wardrobe in Manitoba, Canada, and a wardrobe near Cambridge in England, contained identical dark items of clothing. Even though they were way, way beyond fighting age, two old Nazis, a continent apart, probably unknown to each other, kept their SS uniforms hanging up behind closed doors, waiting for the day when they would be called back into battle. There may have been many more like them – fanatics in reserve.

My dad said of his father: "Once a Nazi, always a Nazi."

When I began researching this book, I wanted to believe that my grandfather, out of barely believable naivety, genuinely did not know what was happening in the concentration camps. Then, as I learned more, I hoped that his broken personality after the war was the result of being overwhelmed by contrition, an almost unbearable guilt at his personal role in the atrocities which had now been laid bare. But I kept coming back to a line from the prosecution case at his tribunal: "The defendant did not show any evidence that after recognising the injustice of the camps, he was in psychological conflict and thus felt the moral duty to withdraw from the organisation".

A professor of religious studies in the US, Katharina von Kellenbach, the niece of a man who had personally ordered the slaughter of thousands in Poland, studied the last words of those condemned to hang in Bavaria's Landsberg prison. These were people who had committed murders, or ordered killings. They were among the worst perpetrators to be brought to trial. If anyone had reason to be weighed down by guilt it was these men and women. One hundred and thirty people guilty of heinous crimes gave a last statement on the scaffold, and not one of them showed any remorse.

In the four years between his capture and execution at Landsberg, Oswald Pohl, the man who exerted total control over the concentration camps, the man who had apparently looked in to watch Jews being gassed, always qualified the word "guilt" in relation to himself with quotation marks. He "found God", giving himself an easy way to get himself automatic absolution and a pure soul without paying penance. Pastor Martin Niemöller, an early supporter and later opponent of Nazism, commented that if the offenders came to address their crimes they would surely hang themselves. Instead, they left it to someone else to put the noose round their necks and died with clear consciences.

An estimated half a million Germans were directly involved in the Holocaust. Half a million. No wonder my uncle Eki's wife Adelheid told me ruefully when I asked her about how she felt about me investigating the family story: "What is there to hide? Just about every family had someone who did something." After the war, nearly all of the perpetrators looked to excuse themselves or blame others. They had to follow orders. They would have been put in a concentration camp if they had objected. Their families would be punished. They were just doing their job. They didn't know what was going on.

I can only conclude, in the absence of any evidence to the contrary, that while my grandfather felt dejection at the outcome – "He was disappointed in Hitler," said my dad – he found the means, like so many others, to justify to himself what he had done.

I set out to find the people behind barbed wire who had any connection with Karl Niemann. There were, of course, thousands of nameless Jews, homosexuals, Jehovah's Witnesses, Sinti and Roma who perished in the camps or on death marches along with their children, and so left no trace.

What about the men whom Karl had had released from concentration camps? Or rather, their surviving offspring, if there were any? Some could not be traced: one would not answer my letters. I respect his silence.

In Vienna, I found (with some help), Xenia Katzenstein, Miss Austria 1963, star of a long-running TV commercial, familiar throughout the German-speaking world a generation ago as Tante Kaffee (Auntie Coffee). In this story, she is better known as Xenia Doppler, daughter of Franz, the engineer arrested by the Gestapo and imprisoned in Dachau.

I was humbled and grateful that Frau Katzenstein responded courteously to my initial letter. But when I went on to ask for information, I got the first inkling of a lifetime of hurt: "You must wait a bit longer for me to answer your questions. It has been a long time since I dealt with the subject of 'Dachau' and 'father'."

Soon after, she wrote back with her memories of the father who had died 60 years before. Xenia Katzenstein was Franz Doppler's second daughter, born a year after he was freed from Dachau. If her father had love for her, said Frau Katzenstein, he never, ever, as far as she could recall, showed it: "He had hardly any emotional or physical connection to the affairs of the family. In photographs of our early childhood, it is always children and wife. He had no body contact with us. My mother said the years in Dachau changed him a great deal. He came back 'different'."

The SS generation who inflicted death and suffering on millions did not, in any meaningful sense, atone for their crimes. And, as Frau Katzenstein and millions of others demonstrate, those crimes left a legacy of pain on the descendants of those who were kept behind barbed wire. Those who bore witness are nearly all dead: some of those in the generations who follow keep memories of the injustices alive.

But what of the families of the guilty, families like mine? Many Germans do not know, or do not want to know, what their forebears did in the war. A former schoolmate said she did not like her cold German grandfather. As for what made him cold – she had no idea. An official in Dachau's tourist information office told me her Austrian grandparents had left the then independent country to embrace the Nazi Party in Bavaria, and that they were "not nice people". How great a distance is it from "cold" or "not nice" to a collaborator, an accomplice, a killer?

My father and his siblings never challenged their mild-mannered, inoffensive, broken-down father, sitting quietly in his chair. I do not think they wanted answers. Dr Jan Erik Schulte, a man who has devoted a lifetime to Holocaust studies, says that it was too painful for the sons and daughters to probe into the guilt of their fathers. Four years ago, my father said: "Quite honestly we don't really know if he did anything bad. We don't know. I mean, as far as I know, he wasn't the one that killed the people. And he might not even have known that they killed the people. He might have wondered that they're not there any more or something like that. But I'm convinced that he just did a good job and that was that."

In the Niemanns' home town of Hameln lives a remarkable man with a history of shame in his family. Retired teacher and historian Bernhard Gelderblom was born during the war in present-day Poland, the son of an SS officer who had been posted there as part of the vicious "Germanisation" of the region. Thirty years ago, he embarked on a project that has come to dominate his life. He wanted to connect his young students from Hameln and the surrounding villages with the Nazi past of the places where they lived and hit on an ingenious way of giving it a meaningful, human dimension. He looked into the still-extant Jewish cemeteries and began to bring the names on the gravestones to life, researching their stories. In one village, the tombstones had been smashed during the Nazi years: he persuaded the people of the village to give their time and money to restoring the cemetery. I asked him what had driven him to dedicate himself in this way:

Why am I doing this work? A trigger was actually my father a long time ago. He was a Nazi, a convinced Nazi and at times a stormtrooper, and later an officer. Without Hitler, he would probably have been unemployed. So I can therefore understand his initial enthusiasm.

What I resented in him is the fact that he learned nothing from the war. He could not think critically about his past and always took a sceptical stance against democracy.

But my father was just the kick-off for me. What then became very important was my work as a teacher. I wanted to show my students that the things that happened in Berlin were also done here in Hameln, and that they were not only happening here because they had been ordered from Berlin, but because they were wanted here. I call my work local history of National Socialism.

I have actually had very good reactions from people when I do guided tours or hold lectures. I'm trying, in what I say, to always make things concrete, to always bring examples of people who could be followed.

Very important drivers for me are also, of course, family members of the persecuted, murdered or displaced. I'm always looking for contact with them, inviting them to Hameln, having a full correspondence with them, providing them with sufficient documents, helping them find the graves of their family members etc. This is very time-consuming work, but for me the most wonderful reward.

Bernhard was goaded by vociferous denials and views that he found abhorrent in his own father. But he grew up after the Nazi regime had worked its poison. What of those who were raised under Hitler?

Anne, the girl who played innocently in pre-war Hameln with her new-found Jewish friends and went so far as to visit them in their homes, was warped through her teenage years and early adulthood by the overwhelming doctrine of anti-Semitic hatred, the sort of hatred that encouraged hundreds to crowd round in the streets to laugh at poor souls on their hands and knees, made to scrub the pavements. Such hateful conditioning never quite left her. As an old lady, she went shopping in cosmopolitan Glasgow with her granddaughters. "Look, that one's a Jew!" she would say, pointing at a figure in the crowd. "Gran!" cried her granddaughters, aghast. "You can't say things like that."

Anne and my dad left a country where there was one kind of virulent prejudice and, by coincidence, landed in a town where there was another. Larkhall has been widely acknowledged as, historically, the most bigoted place in Scotland. The persecution and murder of Jews, homosexuals and other ostracised groups in Nazi Germany cannot, in the scale of suffering, be compared. But both situations are driven by fear of those who are different. People who are unhappy or insecure about their own position in life attack those whom they see as outsiders.

In Hameln, there are real grounds for optimism about the future in people like Bernhard Gelderblom. In Scotland, there are those like Dave Scott. A Northern Irishman who was born a Catholic in Protestant Lisburn, he grew up through the Troubles with his whole life infected by the religious divide. He crossed the Irish Sea and went to university in Stirling to find a wider world. He stood on the terraces at football matches and heard thousands singing in unison: "We're up to our knees in Fenian* blood." "I thought I'd escaped," he said, "but here it was all over again."

Dave's outlet for bringing about change is as campaign director of an organisation called Nil by Mouth. Its aim is to break down sectarianism in Scotland. Sometimes, he goes into schools to preach a message of tolerance: "I want children to be able to say, my pal goes to a Protestant school or my pal goes to a Catholic school. He's still my pal."

The organisation presented its first award to a place which had done the most to counter religious bigotry. It went to Larkhall.

Dave admits that, for all his laudable aims, he will be criticised: "I know that in my work, everything you say you'll be abused for. There are people trying to lean on you." I suggested that his position was extremely tough. "Aye, but at the end of the day, I can leave my job, go home and forget about it. *You* have to live with it."

Kind words, and just as kind as the soft-spoken archivists in Dachau, Sachsenhausen and Berlin's museum of the SS, earnest people who responded with a mantra when I told them of my grandfather's role: "It's not your fault. It's not your fault." But I do not seek personal forgiveness or nurse any self-pity. I was not raised by this man – he was dead before I was born. I do not have the filial bonds that leave my dad and his brother torn by love for their father and uncertainty about what he did. I belong to the generation that

---

* Derogatory slang for Catholic.

247

German historians of the Holocaust have found – within the last few years – is coming to them for answers about their family past.

Two years ago, I went to the concentration camp at Dachau, the pivotal location of this story. In an archive room, two German historians sat opposite me and told me that my grandfather would, without question, have known something about the atrocities that were taking place and that he would have socialised with some of the worst offenders of the Holocaust. Apparently I left the building, apparently I took notes in the doorway and my wife – seeing my face – took my photograph. I have no recollection.

What I do remember is a teenage German girl running from the gas chamber distraught and being comforted outside by her friend. And most of all, I remember feeling both an affinity with and an isolation from the many visitors of all nationalities, who milled around the memorial site. We must all have shared shock and revulsion at what was presented in front of us. But guilt by association made me angry. I of all people knew that most of those who carried out the crimes were not the inherently evil ogres we wanted to believe they were. I wanted to shout: "Don't distance yourselves from this. The people who did this are like me. And like you." And that is the hardest thing to accept and the easiest thing to hide in self-righteous indignation.

I came back to Britain after that revelatory visit to Dachau, and went to see a Jewish friend to confess what I had learned. He shrugged: "People are people." His comment typifies the open-minded response I have encountered from everyone I have spoken to while researching this book. An elderly Jewish lady who had lost family in the Holocaust even apologised for my grandfather: "He probably had no choice." Well, maybe.

Karl Niemann died just at the point when a new movement was emerging in Germany. It was called *Vergangenheitsbewältigung*.

The word translates as "coming to terms with the past". Today, the country still sends its children to concentration camps: now they go to learn from the errors of their forebears. Where flags and banners once shouted triumphalism in the streets of Berlin, there are monuments and display panels, telling, with self-lacerating humility, what Germany did to its own people and to millions of innocents in other lands. There is full acknowledgement among young, middle-aged, even old Germans, who are innocent of crimes that are fast disappearing from living memory.

I have an albatross with a swastika around my neck. Hameliner Bernhard Gelderblom has one too. We must both tell our stories over and over and play a very small part in chasing away the "Nazi" from all of us. It is chastening. But it feels the right thing to do.

A NOTE ON THE PHOTOGRAPHS

When I began work on *A Nazi in the Family*, I knew of only three family photographs in existence covering the period spanned by this book. Within a year, there were more than 400. Most came from two major sources: one was unexpected, the other truly astonishing. The photograph section of this book features a selection of these images, with the background to each detailed in the list below.

Minna and her children came down from their Alpine hideout in 1945 as human packhorses. The two boys were aged eleven and seven; the two women were not exactly muscle-bound. They carried only what they considered to be essentials and those essentials included a stack of photo albums, the only physical and visual memory of the life they had left behind. The pictures made it to a train more than a month later and went with them on the journey back to Hameln.

After her parents' death, Anne took away nearly all of the photographs for herself. She took Dieter's last letters from the front too and hid them inside her passport. Eki was left with a small number – mostly duplicates. Rudi ended up with just two, a wedding photograph of his parents and one of the family bunker (photo no. 20).

Anne hid the photographs away – neither Rudi nor her daughter

Isabelle remembered ever seeing them – until one day in the mid-1980s when Anne's granddaughter Kirsten came home from school with a copy of *When Hitler Stole Pink Rabbit*. Judith Kerr's heartrending story of her Jewish childhood in Berlin and escape from Germany captivated the little girl and prompted her to ask her grandmother about her own childhood in Germany. Anne brought out her albums, but offered glimpses rather than full enlightenment: "She would say a little, and then change the subject suddenly. It was as if going back became too much for her to manage," said Kirsten.

At about the same time, Eki returned for the first time to Berlin, the city of his early childhood. Though he and his second wife Adelheid had gone there as part of a church group visit, Eki took a notion to go off schedule and see his old home in Zehlendorf. The middle-aged man navigated through the eyes of a seven-year-old. All the street names had been changed, so his route was followed by memory.

The couple arrived at the front door of the house and knocked, just as Eki's mother had done more than 30 years before. As in 1955, Frau Schwartz answered the door. However, this was not the woman who had tried to trick Minna, but an Argentinian woman, now living in the house of her recently departed mother-in-law. Frau Schwartz the younger welcomed Eki and his wife into her house. Not much had changed – the great oven was still in the front room, the wood-framed bunk beds were still in the cellar. The woman seemed to be fascinated by Eki's recollections of his life there and, at the end of the visit, they parted with cheery farewells.

A few weeks later, a small package arrived at the Niemanns' house. It had been sent by the woman's husband. Herr Schwartz had been absent when the couple dropped in. He had enclosed a friendly accompanying letter explaining that he had found the contents of the package among his late mother's possessions. It was a packet containing 110 hand-cut photo negatives. Many of the negatives correspond to the prints that the family took to the Alps and then carried back to Hameln. But there are some – politically sensitive and historically important – for which no prints survive. Photos 6, 7 and 10 are part of this remarkable archive. There is every likelihood that the original prints were destroyed by the family after the war. Perhaps they were potentially incriminating, or maybe Minna purged the collection of overtly Nazi content that did not even have the saving grace of depicting her own family.

The big unanswered question is why Frau Schwartz should have kept these negatives for the rest of her life. Why did she not give them back to Minna in 1955? Or why, as a Jewish woman with every reason to feel anger at what she saw, did she not destroy them?

The stories in the pictures

1) Officer cadet Karl Niemann, August 1914

Newly commissioned Karl wearing an officer cadet uniform, most likely pictured in August 1914, during the week he signed up to fight. The epaulette on his left shoulder bears the number of his Hannoverian regiment – 164. The abnormally short fourth and fifth fingers of his left hand show his congenital deformity. The regimental sword he bears was buried at the bottom of a wardrobe during the Second World War.

2) Newly-weds Minna and Karl, c1921

One of a series of studio photographs – perhaps taken for Karl and Minna's wedding in November 1921? Theirs is a relationship that is fundamental to the story.

3) Minna wearing Karl's army tunic, c1916

The principal boy in a pantomime? The smooth-faced youth in the picture is Minna! In all probability, she donned Karl's army officer's tunic and cap for a playful pose while he was on leave from the Western Front (either 1916 or 1917).

4) Anne and Dieter, summer c1930

Anne and Dieter captured on a roadside verge, possibly in the summer of 1930.

5) Anne and Dieter, Dortmund, Christmas 1928

Anne and Dieter: Dortmund, Christmas 1928. There is something beautifully ethereal about the light shining on the little children. And somehow it is a last moment of innocence before the Great Depression of the following year and their father's descent into Nazi Party politics.

6) Army parade, Dortmund, early 1930s

A military parade in Dortmund's market place. This is the sharpest of three photographs taken on that occasion by Karl of the Reichswehr – the forerunner of the Wehrmacht (German army). The absence of swastikas suggests that this is a pre-1933 picture.

7) Stormtrooper rally in Dortmund, c1930

We can get a partial sense of the significance of this stormtrooper parade through Dortmund photographed by Karl if we liken it to a Protestant march through a Catholic district of Belfast at the height of the Troubles. It is a deliberately provocative incursion into another's territory. Only the scene shown here is far more dangerous. This brownshirt parade is passing through a Communist-dominated district in the north of the city. Both Nazis and Communists carried knuckledusters, steel bars and knives to break up marches, and beat up (and sometimes kill) their opponents. Are the people tagging alongside sympathetic or hostile? Is the man at the bottom left with a swagger in his step imitating or mocking the marchers? The passengers on the bus are not looking at the parade. An act of political defiance? In the background, beyond the allotments, we can see the multiple smokestacks of industrial Dortmund.

8) Anne in League of German Girls (BDM) uniform, c1936

Anne in the winter uniform of the Bund Deutscher Mädel (League of German Girls), the female equivalent of the Hitler Youth, c1936. She wears a dark blue skirt, white blouse and a black neckerchief with a leather slide.

9) Karl wearing Nazi Party and SS pin badges, February 1940

Karl adopts a "heroic" pose, looking out into the distance, for an official photo taken on 8th February 1940. On his lapel, he wears a Nazi Party badge and SS insignia. It is at a point when his professional career is at its peak.

10) Arrival of senior SS officer at Dachau Concentration Camp, 1935/6

A snowy scene in the winter of 1935/6. Archivists rate this slightly blurred, grainy picture as being of "high historical interest". It was taken by Karl at Dachau and shows, judging by the number of staff gathered around, what appears to be the visit of a high-ranking SS officer. The group of SS officers in the foreground are clustered around him. As the picture is being taken, the officer on the left of the group is giving the senior officer a *Heil Hitler* salute.

The picture looks out over an open field to the *Geisterwald* (ghost forest) planted during World War One, and then beyond towards the city of Dachau, which rises in the distance. At that time, the concentration camp was still some distance from the city. In 1936, the Eickeplatz estate (named after the infamous *Kommandant*) was built in the field, the start of an urbanisation that has left today's concentration camp surrounded by housing.

New SS recruit Karl may have taken this shot illicitly or surreptitiously – it was certainly an important occasion in his mind. The photograph gives a rare glimpse into the workings of the SS from an insider's point of view. Karl took it from the upstairs window of the guardhouse at the entrance to the SS training camp. It is the exact location of today's concentration camp visitor centre.

11) Karl in Nazi Party uniform, Dortmund, 1933

Oliver Hardy or Nazi enforcer? Karl wears his Nazi Party uniform and the lapels denoting a block warden. The uniform of a lowly official does not tally with Karl's wartime records in which he stated he was a block leader by 1932. His swastika-armbanded arm is around Minna, pregnant with Rudi late in the summer of 1933. The photographer has forgotten to take his own shadow into account.

12) SS social outing, Bavaria, c1937

An SS officers' day trip to the Alps in the summer of 1937. The lederhosen-clad men and their wives (Karl and Minna second and third from the left) are sitting on the terrace of a bar with icons of the age plastered on the wall behind them, indications that they are drinking outside a bastion of Nazism. A framed photograph of Hitler from the Nazi newspaper the *Völkischer Beobachter* is above an advert for an *Almtanz*, a popular dance to mark the pre-autumn movement of cattle down from the mountains. The archway door carries an advert for a showing of Leni Riefenstahl's film *Triumph of the Will*. Immediately below, a theatre production of *Der Siebte Bua* (Bavarian dialect for *The Seventh Boy*) is promoted. Above Karl's head is an advert for the *Reiter-korps* (the Nazi rider corps, founded in 1936). Far left, the blackboard is titled D.A.F. – the initials of the state-controlled labour organisation that replaced all trade unions. The brewery sign far right hints that this might be the town of Traunstein, close to the Austrian border.

13) *The Nazi Party! New Year celebrations, Berlin, 1939*

A drunken celebration at the Niemanns' to mark New Year's Day, 1939 (Karl is third from the right, Minna second from the left, toasting the woman beside her). At one level, this is comically absurd – a bunch of revellers schnapped by the photographer looking much the worse for wear, festooned with streamers, some with party hats, the lady sitting at the front wearing a 1939 crown, a mawkish picture of kittens on the wall. But there is a sinister undertone. The men in uniform are police lieutenants (one beheaded by the camera) and both the man on the far right making eyes at his neighbour and the fez-wearing moustached man seated second from the left are wearing SS pin badges. Since both SS and police officers were allowed to live in the SS-camaraderie settlement of Krumme Lanke, these may well be immediate neighbours invited in for a New Year's house-warming party.

14) *Karl and Eki, Berlin, 1938/9*

Intimate picture of Karl with his infant son, Eki, taken shortly after the family moved to Berlin (either late 1938 or early 1939).

15) *Father and son, Berlin, 1938/9*

The body language seems to epitomise the often difficult relationship between Karl and Dieter. Scaffolding around the house in the background and the bare ground at their feet are strong evidence that this picture was taken in the winter of 1938/9, while the SS estate was still being built.

16) Minna, Rudi and Eki, c1943

Minna's two youngest boys had a very close relationship with their mother. Even as a teenager, Eki would sit on his mother's knee for comfort after the end of a love affair. In this picture from 1943 or 1944, little Eki plays to the camera, while Rudi is sullen and unresponsive.

17) Family and friends, summer 1939

Minna and her children with unknown friends in the back garden of Dienstweg in the summer of 1939. Minna holds her youngest boys close, Eki fiddling with Dieter's Hitler Youth shoulder strap. Anne has a wardrobe malfunction with her BDM uniform.

18) Minna and Dieter, c1942

Mother and son in Berlin, 1942. Had Dieter been wearing a Scout uniform, there would be nothing exceptional in this picture of a loving mother and her eldest son. But the photo jars because Dieter is wearing his summer service Hitler Youth uniform. A triangular badge on Dieter's left sleeve indicates the Berlin district to which he belonged.

19) Eki with the family silver, 1944

Eki's twice-daily trek to the air raid shelter at the bottom of the garden carrying the family silver is captured on camera. He is standing immediately in front of the bunker.

20) *The family bunker, Berlin, 1944*

Women and children pose at the air raid bunker in the summer of 1944. Karl and Dieter are probably both away at work. The three women next to Eki (far left) were the family's neighbours and bunker companions. The young woman in the check dress in front of Minna and Rudi was Grete, the Niemanns' maid (*Dienstmädchen*). This picture was probably taken in the low sun of the morning – American bombers would have been expected towards lunchtime or late afternoon. There would not, however, have been a heightened sense of fear at this time, for there was only sporadic bombing that summer.

21) *First day at Panzer school, November 1944*

Dropping-off day at Panzer school, Neuruppin, November 1944. Dieter (far left) wears his Hitler Youth winter uniform. Karl (centre) is the dominant figure in this picture.

22) *Military training camp, 1942*

One of three surviving photographs taken by an inexperienced photographer (most likely Dieter) who failed to grasp the basics of a contemporary twin reflex camera, and so managed to chop off both heads and feet. The Hitler Youth boys in the picture are at a Wehrertüchtigungslager (military training competency camp) in 1942.

23) *Dieter in uniform (with SS flashes obliterated), 1945*

This late photograph taken of Dieter (wearing the uniform of a Waffen SS private) hung in the Hameln living room above Karl's chair. In her book *Photography and Death*, Audrey Linkman writes: "For those without a grave to visit… the photograph in the home became the focus of mourning." The inset shows how the picture has been doctored. Using a pencil, Minna very carefully obliterated the SS runes on Dieter's lapel and made the photograph acceptable for post-war display.

24) Rudi and Eki fraternising with the enemy, Spring 1945

German children crowd round a camera for their picture in US-occupied Alpine Schliersee, just after the German surrender in May 1945. Eki (second from right) wears a paper hat. Rudi has a soldier's helmet, but whose helmet? Look carefully and you can see that he is perching on a seated American soldier's leg. And next to his left shoulder you can see the soldier's face. Eki thinks that the three girls in the photo are Heinke, Anke and Elke – the daughters of fanatical Nazi parents, who accompanied them from Berlin to the Alps. This is the only photograph from that turbulent period.

25) Downtime at Anne's wedding, Hameln, 1947

An off-guard moment outside Hameln's Münsterkirche, at the wedding of Anne and Corporal George Falconer in June 1947. After the formal ceremony of the wedding itself, the position of hands and fingers suggests that we are now at the stress-relieving handing-out of cigarettes. Rudi and Eki are standing in front of Anne (second from right). Mimi Schwenker, the sister-in-law who turned the family away from the door when they returned to Hameln after the war, is on the far left of the picture. Only two years before, the young men in uniform were the enemy.

26) The Niemann family, Hameln, 1950

There are echoes of nineteenth century practices of honouring the dead in this photograph from November 1950. The person who dominates the picture is not even there. Audrey Linkman writes: "Photographs or other representations of the dead were sometimes introduced into the portraits of the living to indicate that, though absent, the deceased were not forgotten... Many bereaved sitters preferred to be photographed holding a portrait of the deceased ... to demonstrate their constancy and love for the absent person." The two boys, all youthful promise, pose with their dead brother's picture between them. There is a stark contrast between the boys and the three troubled adults in front of them. Anne, by now living in Scotland, looks older than her 27 years. It was on this first return to Hameln that she announced she was staying in Germany... but her father ordered her to go back to her husband.

27) Minna, Karl and mysterious friend, Hameln 1959

In the couple's last summer, Karl had just enough mobility to take him, with the help of a walking stick, a short distance down the Weser to a riverside café. There would be nothing exceptional about this picture, except that a stamp on the back reveals it was developed in Schliersee, Bavaria. So just who is the man sitting with them at the table? An old SS comrade?

28) Rudi's family, Glasgow, 1963

Goosesteps come to Glasgow. A very ordinary family in a city suburb in 1963. The budgie in the cage above answers to the name of Eki. The ruddy-cheeked author is on his mother's knees. Rudi has a very German-looking haircut.

29) Three little braves, Glasgow, 1965

Three little cousins in a Cambuslang garden, dressed in native American costume made for them by Eki. L to R: Martin, Michael (Eki's son), Derek.

30) Front Cover Image

Karl does some early-evening gardening – still wearing his office clothes. The three pips of a *Hauptsturmführer* (captain) are visible on his lapels, as is the Iron Cross on his left pocket and the ribbons of the Cross of Honour. Perhaps jodhpurs are not the ideal attire for sweeping leaves into a fire. But maybe Karl would cut an ordinary figure here – an SS officer on an SS estate in Berlin. The likely date for this photo is May 1944.

All the images that appear in this book have been carefully digitally restored, primarily to improve tone and contrast and to remove minor physical damage such as spots and scratches, to ensure that they were suitable for publication. Some images have been lightly cropped to fit.

Identification of dates and individuals has depended on information from a number of sources. These include whatever is written on the reverse of the images, the location, the apparent age of the children, information from uniforms and the like, and witness testimony from Rudi and Ekart.

Nothing has been digitally removed from, or inserted into, any of the images. They are a faithful record of the images taken by members of the Niemann family.

Appendix

The court judgment against Karl Niemann, July 1948
(reproduced with kind permission of the Niedersächsisches
Landesarchiv, Hauptstaatsarchiv Hannover)

JUDGMENT
In the name of the people!

In the denazification trial
versus
bank clerk and former captain of the Allgemeine and
Waffen SS Karl Niemann from Hameln, born
30.4.1893 in Hemeringen,
the number 12 court in Stade in the sitting from 8th July 1948, in
which participated: Senior Judge Schulz as the
chair, farmer Gustav Kolster, as a member of the
committee, the first lawyer Dr Bischoff, and Justice
Töpser as the clerk of the office

has declared the following:

the defendant is sentenced to one year in prison for his membership
of the Allgemeine and Waffen SS; he also has to cover the fee of the

trial. The sentence counts, however, as fulfilled, as he has already spent time in prison.

The defendant living in Hameln became, after high school, a bank clerk. From 1914, he took part in the First World War, as a volunteer. In 1916, he was promoted to lieutenant, and was, from 1917–1920, in France as a prisoner of war. After his release, he worked for the Deutsche Bank, and various industrial firms. From 1934–1935, he worked full time as a local group finance manager of the DAF in Dortmund.

On 1.1.1931, he became a member of the NSDAP and was from 1932–1935 a Block Leader.

From 1.11.1935, he belonged to the Allgemeine SS in which he reached the rank of SS captain. On 1.11.1935, he became, as a civil employee, an auditor of the economic enterprises of the SS in Dachau, which were at that time under the control of the SS Munich. He was, as auditor of these firms, personally responsible to SS-Gruppenführer Pohl. In 1938, he was then transferred to the Business and Administration Office of the SS in Berlin, where he worked as the chair of the department and deputy acting director in office W4. This office was mainly responsible for wood and metal processing factories (DAW).

All of which were located in proximity to concentration camps and employed camp prisoners. The defendant worked in office W4, which was purely economic, until the collapse.*

He was general manager of the Deutsche Ausrüstungswerke GmbH Berlin, of the German Meisterwerkstätten GmbH in Prag, and executive member of the German Edelmöbel AG in Butschewitz near Brünn, all of which were owned by the SS. In the two

---

* *Zusammenbruch* – the collapse marking the end of the war.

last-named firms, only civilians were employed. From 1935–1942, the defendant was a lieutenant in the Wehrmacht. In 1942, he was transferred from the Wehrmacht to the Waffen SS, and referred to as a captain. He remained, however, in his position in the WVHA. In the Waffen SS, he held the rank of captain. On 9.5.45, the Americans arrested him as a prisoner of war in Bavaria (where he had been transferred as part of his work).

The defendant is married, and father of four children aged 9–24. He left the church in 1936 or 1937. He is as yet unpunished. He was imprisoned until 11.3.48 when he was released on the basis of the *Beurlaubungsaktion*.*

The prosecution charges that because he had been since 1.9.1939 a member of the Allgemeine and Waffen SS, he had knowledge of the fact that these organisations were used for acts that count (according to… order 69 of the Nuremberg Judgment) as criminal offences.

It is clear that the defendant had been since 1.11.35 a member of the Allgemeine SS (and in the end held the rank of SS captain) and since 1942 a member of the Waffen SS. He belongs therefore to a group of people who count as criminals (according to article 6 of the [Status IMG] and order 69 of the Nuremberg Judgment).

With respect to the group of people responsible for the prosecution of political opponents, the defendant knew of most of the concentration camps from his own experience. While working in Dachau from 1935–1938, he watched the camp prisoners at work. He also did so while he was a member of the WVHA and on numerous business trips (to do auditing work for the DAW) to the concentration camps of Auschwitz, Buchenwald, Dachau, Lemberg, Lublin, Neuengamme, Ravensbrück, Sachsenhausen and Stutthof.

---

* A special leave of absence granted to internees.

He saw and talked to the prisoners there. He knew that in these camps were primarily political prisoners who were active against the regime, and that a smaller number of inmates were professional criminals, anti-social elements, Bible researchers and persons who violated § 175 of the German Penal Code. He knew that some of the political opponents were only imprisoned there because of their political convictions. The same applied to Jews, who were often only arrested because of their race. The Bible researchers were put in a camp because of communistic propaganda.

With respect to the anti-social elements, he knew of a case in which a particular individual was sent to a camp for some time for educational reasons. When clergymen gave politically critical speeches they were, according to his knowledge, also sent to a camp. He knew from conversations that clergymen and priests worked in the herb garden in Dachau. He knew that war criminals, Jews and Poles, who worked in the nearby DAW, were imprisoned in the camps in Lublin and Lemberg. The defendant had knowledge that the incarceration happened in most cases without judicial judgment. He knew furthermore that in the course of time, immigrants were also among the camp prisoners. But he did not know that they were given special treatment.

The defendant did not witness abuse of the camp prisoners. He did know, however, that prisoners who were unwilling to work and those who committed a serious offence were beaten, and that the block leader beat people up from time to time. In the factories of which he was in charge, he never noticed that prisoners were absent due to weakness or maltreatment. He knew about the order from Pohl, head of the WVHA, from 30.4.42 – 110 – concerning the unlimited work time of the prisoners in the camps. In factories of the DAW that he managed, working prisoners received until 1943 a daily extra ration of 200g of bread and 100g of sausage. The fatalities in Dachau concentration camp were, according to his knowledge, about fifteen per quarter year. He said he found this out by the number of coffins that were made. He said he never heard about facilities in the camps for cremating people or about gas chambers. He said he did not know of the "special treatment" and executions of prisoners, or Himmler's decree from 6.1.43 (GJ 117) about medical experiments on prisoners.

The defendant thus had according to his own account, extensive knowledge about the fact that political opponents were randomly and arbitrarily sent to the camps only because of their political convictions. Furthermore, he knew that Jews were sent there because of their race, and clergymen, priests and Bible researchers because of their religious convictions. He knew that most of those who were sent to camps were there without any assurance of an orderly judicial process, and thereby lost their freedom for years and became exposed to the despotism of the camp leader and the camp guards.

Even if the defendant did indeed not know about the atrocities such as the hanging, the gassing, the executions by firing squad, he still knew according to his own confessions about the inhumane treatment of the camp prisoners, in particular about the fact that beatings were used not only as a disciplinary measure and that prisoners had to work with insufficient food until exhaustion.

That this kind of transfer of people to the camps and the inhumane treatment of the inmates constitutes a crime against humanity goes without saying. The defendant was fully aware of the injustice of these measures because he did not deny his own responsibility from the beginning.

He also confessed that he did reflect on the whole system of the camps, but suggested that if he had said or done something, he would possibly have been sent to a camp himself. But he did not explain why, given his knowledge about all this, he had never had any wish to withdraw from his organisation.

The transferral of immigrants to the camps without orderly judicial processes and the incarceration of Polish and Jewish war prisoners in the camps and their being forced to work in the factories of the DAW are also a crime against humanity or to be considered a war crime. All of which, the defendant knew about.

According to his own confession, the defendant also knew that office group D of the SS WVHA was responsible for the administration of the camps and the SS associations that guarded the camps. Therewith he knew that the SS was used to persecute people for political, racial and religious reasons and to put immigrants and prisoners of war into the camps.

Not only can we ascribe to him the crimes committed by the Allgemeine SS and the Waffen SS, but also the acts of other SS formations , because the SS is, according to the Nuremberg Judgment, to be considered one organisational unity.

It is thus shown that the defendant knew enough – about the persecution of people for political, racial, and religious reasons, about the transfer of civilians from occupied areas, and of war criminals to the camps, and the use of the SS for those criminal measures – for him to be convicted.

With respect to the group of people responsible for the persecution of the Jews, the defendant knew about the Nuremberg laws.[*] About the incidents of the *Kristallnacht*, he learned later. But he claims not to have known of the involvement of the SS. He knew that the Jews were ordered to pay a fine of one billion Reichmarks. He also knew that Jews left Germany and during the war were

---

[*] Laws passed in 1935 that deprived Jews of German citizenship and imposed other economic and social restrictions.

deported to the east. He claims he did not know about the destination of these transports and about the fate of the Jews in the east.

These partial confessions of the defendant are sufficient for his conviction. Because according to the report of the police president from Berlin from 13.9.47, in the years 1941 to March 1945, ongoing deportations of Jews were taking place in Berlin. And the defendant confessed that it is possible that he knew about the involvement of the SS in the collection of the Jews from their flats and workplaces (with lorries). Since the defendant lived in Berlin from 1936–1945 continuously, and worked there for the WVHA (of the SS) in a leading position, it can be assumed with absolute certainty that he knew about these deportations and the strong participation of the SS as guards of the lorries, because they were, according to the police president in Berlin and his report, part of everyday conversations.

The submission by the defendant that he visited Lemberg and Lublin only briefly a few times, and apart from that never spent time in occupied areas in the east and thus did not know anything about the mass executions of the Jews in the east could not be contradicted in the oral proceedings.

That the forced deportation of the Jews from Berlin represented a crime against humanity needs no supporting evidence. It is thus shown that the defendant also knew about the group of people responsible for the persecution of the Jews and the participation of the SS in these criminal measures. And this knowledge is incriminating.

The assumption of distress is out of the question; because the defendant did not show any evidence that after recognising the injustice of the camps, he was in psychological conflict and thus felt the moral duty to withdraw from the organisation. Whether the defendant knew about more crimes against humanity could not be proven during the oral proceedings.

It was thus found that with respect to the group responsible for the persecution of people for political, racial, and religious reasons, the persecution of the Jews, and the transport of civilians from occupied areas and war criminals to camps, the defendant had incriminating knowledge of the criminal use of his organisation.

Despite his knowledge of these crimes against humanity, the defendant stayed after 1.9.39 in the Allgemeine SS and Waffen SS. He is thus (based on the Nuremberg Judgment in conjunction with control law number 10) guilty and is (according to article IV u. V. of the VO 69) to be punished.

As for the punishment, it was aggravating that the defendant remained a member of the Allgemeine SS for ten years and the Waffen SS for three years. Because of his membership, his rank of captain (in a main office of the SS), and his being a deputy acting director (of an office group), he significantly supported the criminal potential of his organisation.

It was also aggravating to the sentence that the defendant had close relations with numerous camps and thus had extensive knowledge of inhumane conditions that existed in them.

Apart from that, the oral proceedings did not bring to light anything negative about the defendant. The prisoners' declarations and police reports from Dachau and Dortmund show that his personal behaviour was impeccable, and that he was not politically active. The declarations of four former camp prisoners speak particularly in the defendant's defence. The declaration of the professor of the institute of technology in Vienna, Dr Doppler (who was released from Dachau concentration camp in 1942) shows that even though Doppler did not know whether the defendant was involved in his release, he had never heard about the defendant being involved in anything harmful to the prisoners. Further statutory declarations by councillor Müller-Strobl, (from Klagenfurt), trader Steiner (from Salzburg), and the part-owner of the company "Orplid" F.W.

Naupold (from Hamburg-Bergedorf) show that the defendant was called "Papa Niemann" by prisoners in Sachsenhausen because of his benevolent behaviour and willingness to help. The defendant managed, after an effort that took one year, to get Naupold released from Sachsenhausen concentration camp. This saved Naupold's life, because he was in such a weak physical state that he would not have lived for another six months. The defendant wasn't able to achieve Steiner's release, because his political offence weighed too heavily on him.

But he also managed to get Müller-Strobl released from the Dachau camp through a service obligation. Furthermore, according to Müller-Strobl, during 1942–1945, the defendant issued "uncountable" release requests for political prisoners; some of them became, after their release was approved, fully paid free employees of the factories that they had worked for. They thus, according to Müller-Strobl, owe their freedom to the defendant as well. According to Müller-Strobl's account, the defendant also prevented him from being sent back to a camp in 1943.

The behaviour of the defendant allows the conclusion that despite his constant contact with the camps, he remained a humane person. According to Müller-Strobl, he had already realised back then that the camp system would lead to the downfall of the German people.

Furthermore, because the defendant also did not make an unfavourable impression in oral proceedings and also overall held to the truth, a prison term of one year as atonement appears – despite his extensive knowledge of the system of the camps and in consideration of his tolerant behaviour toward the prisoners – to be sufficient and apt.

According to § 38 Abs. 2. Verf. O. § 60 of the Code of Criminal Procedure, the time already spent in prison is counted toward the sentence, and the length of this time already fully offsets the sentence.

The decision on the fine rests on § 40 Verf. O. § 465 of the Code of Criminal Procedure.

Signed: Schulz.

Denazification court, Stade

ACKNOWLEDGEMENTS

"I have found it very hard to read this... but it is all true! You must tell everything, the good and the bad." – Ekart Niemann (after reading the manuscript of A Nazi in the Family*)*

At Dachau concentration camp, archivist Albert Knoll greets and assists many, many relatives of the victims. It seemed I was an exceptional visitor: "It is very seldom that we see members of the SS families. It is a taboo – they do not want to speak about what their forebears did. They do not want to know, in case there was anything bad."

And so I owe a special debt of gratitude to all of the Niemanns who trusted in me to open the family vault, and who had the courage to accept me laying bare the uncomfortable truths that might lie within. I owe special thanks to my uncle, Ekart "Eki" Niemann, who, in his late seventies, willingly dredged up the past with full awareness of its implications. He was assisted by my aunt, Adelheid Haller-Niemann, who transcribed every one of his memories.

Thanks also to "Faither", Rudi Niemann, who turned a key in his mind and opened a door into his childhood. He also gave frank (and often funny) recollections of his bizarre early years in Scotland, helped by my mum, May. Much of the detail of Aunt Anne's life came from my cousin Isabelle, who spoke openly about her unhappy mother. Daughters Kirsten Gilmour and Stephanie Farquharson added additional illuminating anecdotes.

The archivists of the concentration camps deserve special praise. How do they cope when their daily working lives are soaked in a cruel kind of insanity? Dachau's Albert Knoll told me: "I am a historian. I must be professional. But when I see the photographs, the films... it is hard." Albert was of great help, as was his colleague Dirk Riedel.

Elsewhere, Dr Jan Erik Schulte, lately of the Hannah Arendt Institut in Dresden, gave me more than an hour of his time, more than 60 minutes of extraordinary insight. Andreas Ehresmann of the Gedenkstätte Neuengamme, Dr Astrid Ley at Sachsenhausen, Dr Harry Stein at Buchenwald, and Ulrich Tempel of the Stiftung Topographie des Terrors in Berlin, made significant contributions. Daniel Uziel of Yad Vashem, Szymon Kowalski at Auschwitz, and Ron Coleman and Noemi Szekely-Popescu of the United States Holocaust Memorial Museum kindly sought after what could not be found in their records.

A number of archivists from other institutions gave assistance. Among them, Andreas Bräunling of the Dachau Stadtarchiv was cheerfully outstanding, giving crucial leads and guidance. Thanks also to Doris Fürstenberg, Kulturamt Steglitz-Zehlendorf; Martin Boswell and Stephen Walton of the Imperial War Museum; Florian Weiss at the Allied Museum, Berlin; Markus Günnewig, Stadtarchiv Dortmund; Karin Schaper, Landkreis Hameln-Pyrmont; Silke Schulte, Stadt Hameln Stadtarchiv; Silvia Schmidt, Bundesarchiv Berlin-Lichterfelde; staff of the Niedersächsisches Landarchiv, Hauptstaatarchiv Hannover, Staatsarchiv München and National Archives at College Park, Maryland; Heinz Dorsch of the Seinsheim tourist information office; Angelika Schmidt at the Deutsche Dienststelle WASt. Hans Bresgott of Factsandfiles.com unearthed SS files in Berlin relating to Karl Niemann.

There were certain key individuals in Germany and Austria. Hameln brought out the remarkable Bernhard Gelderblom, offspring of an SS officer, open-hearted historian of the Jewish experience in the town. Jörg Meyer's research into Karl Niemann's regiment was invaluable in tracking his First World War story. Xenia Katzenstein told me what she remembered of what Dachau had done to her father. Elke Barbera knows Karl Niemann's house in Berlin better than anyone – she lives there. Both she and her father helped me make sense of that former SS estate. Dr Harry Wersenger and Elisabeth Lehmann were able to translate Dieter's letters from the front, written in the *sütterlin* script that is impenetrable to younger Germans. "Jodler" Peppi Eckmair recalled the end of the war in Alpine Schliersee.

In Britain, historian and writer Roger Moorhouse unwittingly triggered this whole thing off with his insightful book on wartime Berlin. Martin Davidson, who also had an SS grandfather, encouraged me to go ahead. Other offspring of German parents were generous with their experiences, especially Horst Yarrow and his sister Karin Pearson. Thanks to their mother Eva for giving her memories too. Charles Tamlyn offered a Welsh perspective on lederhosen.

German tutor Uwe Peters did far more than I paid him for in translating the legalese of the court judgment and became absorbed in the story, as well as correcting my distinctly shaky German. Dave Scott at the anti-sectarian organisation Nil by Mouth inspired me with his passion and commitment to a vital cause. Tamar Drukker translated the oral account from Hebrew of Sachsenhausen inmate Yosef Schwartz. Her husband Robin Standring not infrequently provided reassuring lunchtime bridges between Jew and Gentile. Lucy Christopher offered her house and generous spirit as I began writing this book.

I thank my publisher Short Books for believing in me with this second book and, in particular, Aurea Carpenter and Paul Bougourd. My ex-editor at the *Guardian*, Celia Locks, former RSPB colleagues Mark Boyd and Irene Allen and my son Mike Parry read through the manuscript and tightened up words, sentences and meanings.

Various individuals produced shafts of enlightenment: Martin Howlett, Paul Taylor, Sally Nowell, Helen Macdonald, Vanessa Rashbrook, Elsie Adler, and Paul Grant of St Ninian's, Stonehouse.

Most of all, I acknowledge the person who probably spent as much time working on this book as I did. All of the scratched, faded, chemically disfigured prints and negatives appearing here and used as part of my research – more than 400 in total – were restored by my wife Sarah. She wishes to thank her photo mentor Kay Goddard, conservator Susie Clark and Dr Michael Pritchard of the Royal Photographic Society. There were areas of study that Sarah alone carried out to provide background and supporting material. And throughout the whole process she was my constant unpaid consultant.

There were times when I wanted to hate my grandfather and times when I wanted him to be a hero. But all along she guided me into staying detached and resisting mood swings as new evidence appeared. "Follow the facts," she said, again and again. You, the reader, can judge if I have succeeded.

Derek Niemann
www.whispersfromthewild.co.uk

Bibliography

Allen, William Sheridan, *The Nazi Seizure of Power* (Eyre & Spottiswoode, 1966)

Beevor, Antony, *Berlin: The Downfall 1945* (Penguin Books, 2002)

Benz, Wolfgang and Distel, Barbara, *Der Ort des Terrors: Geschichte des national-sozialistichen Konzentrationslager* (Verlag Beck, 2005)

Bezirksamt Steglitz-Zehlendorf, *Hitlers Schreibtischtäter: das SS-Amt Unter den Eichen* (Westkreuz-Druckerei Ahrens AG, 2013)

Biddiscombe, Perry, *The Denazification of Germany: a history 1945–50* (Tempus Publishing, 2007)

Bielenberg, Christabel, *The Past is Myself* (Chatto & Windus, 1968)

Caplan, Jane, and Wachsmann, Nikolaus (eds), *Concentration Camps in Nazi Germany, the New Histories* (Routledge, 2010)

Costello, John, *Love, Sex & War: changing values 1939–45* (Collins, 1985)

Crew, David F. (ed), *Nazism and German Society 1933–1945* (Routledge, 1994)

Daly, Hugh C. and United States Army, "42nd 'Rainbow' Infantry Division: a combat history of World War II" (1946). *World War Regimental Histories*. Book 64. http://digicom.bpl.lib.me.us/ww_reg_his/64

Dearn, Alan, *The Hitler Youth 1933–45* (Osprey Publishing, 2006)

Distel, Barbara, and Jakusch, Ruth, *Concentration Camp Dachau 1933–1945* (Comité International de Dachau, 1978)

Dortmund unterm Hakenkreuz (www.dortmund.de)

Ehresmann, Andreas, *Die frühe Nachkriegsnutzung des Kriegsgefangenen- und KZ-Auffanglagers Sandbostel unter besonderer Betrachtung des britischen No. 2 Civil Internment Camp Sandbostel* (Beitrage zur Geschichte der national sozialistichen Verfolgung in Norddeutschland, Heft 12, KZ-Gedenkstätte Neuengamme, 2010)

Evans, Richard J., *The Coming of the Third Reich* (Penguin, 2004)

Evans, Richard J., *The Third Reich in Power* (Penguin, 2006)

Evans, Richard J., *The Third Reich at War* (Penguin, 2009)

Friedrich, Reinhold, *Spuren des Nationalsozialismus im bayerischen Oberland: Schliersee und Hausham zwischen 1933 und 1945* (Books on Demand GmbH, 2011)

Gelderblom, Bernard, *Die 50er Jahre in Hameln. Von der harten Mühsam und vom frohen Schaffen der Aufbaujahre* (Niemayer, Hameln, 2008)

Gellately, Robert, *Backing Hitler: consent and coercion in Nazi Germany* (Oxford University Press, 2001)

Gilbert, Martin, *First World War* (Weidenfeld & Nicolson, 1994)

Gilbert, Martin, *The Second World War: a complete history* (Weidenfeld & Nicolson, 1989, reprint Phoenix, 2009)

Goldensohn, Leon, *The Nuremberg Interviews: conversations with the defendants and witnesses* (Pimlico, 2006)

Goldhagen, Daniel Jonah, *Hitler's Willing Executioners: ordinary Germans and the Holocaust* (Abacus, 1996)

Headquarters 36th Infantry Division, US Army, Operations in Germany and Austria 1–10 May 1945, Division Narrative and Statistics (National Archives, Maryland, US)

History of the 42nd Division for the month of April 1945 (National Archives, Maryland, US)

Holocaust Education and Archive Research Team (www.holocaustresearch-project.org)

Höss, Rudolf, *Commandant of Auschwitz*, introduced by Primo Levi (Phoenix Press, 2000)

Kaienburg, Hermann, *Die Wirtschaft der SS* (Metropol, 2003)

Kellenbach, Katharina von, *The Mark of Cain: guilt and denial in the post-war lives of Nazi perpetrators* (Oxford University Press, 2013)

Kershaw, Ian, *The End: Germany 1944–45* (Penguin Books, 2012)

Klemperer, Victor, *I Will Bear Witness: a diary of the Nazi years* (translation: Random House, 1999)

Klotzbach, Kurt, *Gegen den Nationalsozialismus: Widerstand und Verfolgung in Dortmund 1930–1945* (Verlag für Literatur und Zeitgeschehen, 1969)

Koehl, Robert Lewis, *The SS: a history 1919–45* (Tempus Publishing, 1989)

Linkman, Audrey, *Photography and Death* (Reaktion Books, 2011)

Landesdenkmalamt, *Berlin Waldsiedlung Krumme Lanke: untere denkmalschutzbehörde Steglitz-Zehlendorf* (Gagfah, 2006)

Marcuse, Harold, *Legacies of Dachau: the uses and abuses of a concentration camp, 1933–2001* (Cambridge University Press, 2001)

Meyer, Jörg, *Das 4.Hannoversche Infanterie-Regiment Nr.164* (www.hamelner-geschichte.de)

Moorhouse, Roger, *Berlin at War: life and death in Hitler's capital 1939–45* (The Bodley Head, 2010)

Moosburg Online (www.moosburg.org)

Naasner, Walter, *SS-Wirtschaft und SS-Verwaltung* (Droste Verlag, 1998)

Nuremberg Trials Project, a digital document (Harvard Law School Library, 2011)

Orlow, Dietrich, *The History of the Nazi Party 1919–1933* (University of Pittsburgh Press, 1969)

Pflanz, Heinrich, *Das Internierungslager Moosburg 1945–1948* (Landsberg, 1992)

Priemel, Kim, and Stiller, Alexa (eds), *Reassessing the Nuremberg Military Tribunals: transitional justice, trial narratives and histiography* (Berghahn Books, 2012)

Richardi, Hans-Günter, *Dachau: a Guide to its Contemporary History* (City of Dachau, 2001)

Riedel, Dirk, *Ordnungshüter und Massenmörder im Dienst der "Volksgemeinschaft": Der KZ-Kommandant Hans Loritz* (Metropol Verlag, 2010)

Schulte, Jan Erik, *Zwangsarbeit und Vernichtung: Das Wirtschaftsemporium der SS* (Ferdinand Schöningh, 2001)

Shirer, William L., *The Rise and Fall of the Third Reich* (Mandarin, 1960)

Taylor, Frederick, *Exorcising Hitler: the occupation and denazification of Germany* (Bloomsbury, 2011)

Texas Military Forces Museum, *The Story of the 36th Infantry Division* (www.texasmilitaryforcesmuseum.org)

Thad Allen, Michael, *The Business of Genocide: The SS, Slave Labor and the Concentration Camps* (University of North Carolina Press, 2012)

United States Holocaust Memorial Museum (www.ushmm.org)

University of Georgia School of Law, Phillips Nuremberg Trials Collections (http://digitalcommons.law.uga.edu/nuremberg/)

Weber-Newth, Inge, and Steinert, Johannes-Dieter, *German Migrants in Post-war Britain: an enemy embrace* (Routledge, 2006)

Williamson, Gordon, *Panzer Crewman 1939–45* (Osprey Publishing, 2002)

INDEX

קיינמאָל מער
PLUS JAMAIS
NEVER AGAIN
NIE WIEDER
НИКОГДА БОЛЬШЕ